flowers
A *to* Z

Buying
Growing
Cutting
Arranging

Cecelia Heffernan

Photography by T. K. Hill

Harry N. Abrams, Inc., Publishers

Contents

Knowing Flowers

Flowers are an integral part of our life. We celebrate, mourn, and love with them. They talk for us, teach us, comfort us.

Flowers have the power to evoke emotions and memories. They captivate us with their endless diversity of color, shape, size, and fragrance. Yet for many of us, they remain designated for special occasions.

FLOWERS A TO Z dispels the notion that flowers are a luxury rather than a necessity. This book seeks to change the way we think of them. Its principal objective is to bring the enjoyment of flowers into everyday life, whether through arranging cut flowers, growing flowers, or simply appreciating flowers.

FLOWERS A TO Z is based on flowers in their pure and simple state, with facts about each individual kind. It explains how to choose the best cut flowers and to care for them properly, for by prolonging their life, including them in everyday living becomes a practical reality and joy.

hardware

1. Floral shears are used for cutting most flower stems. The blades should be thin and very sharp, to make a clean cut. Do not use standard scissors to cut your flowers: They have thicker blades and will close the stem partway when cut, impairing the absorption of water.

2. Floral shears with long, thin blades are useful for trimming flowers and stems in bouquets, or cutting flowers from the garden in hard-to-reach places. These should be very sharp as well, to make a clean cut.

3. Floral pruning shears are used for cutting thick, fibrous stems, and for thin, woody stems such as azaleas, hydrangeas, etc. The blades should be sharp and able to penetrate the stem and make a clean cut.

4. Heavy-duty pruning shears are used to cut and split thick branches.

5. A hammer is used to split woody stems and branches.

6. A stem stripper is used to clean leaves, thorns, and small branches from the main stem. Be careful not to strip and bruise the main stem, which would shorten the life of the flower by contaminating the water with debris.

7. A floral or paring knife is used to trim thorns, leaves, and small branching stems from the main stem. The knife can also be used to cut the end of stems at an angle.

8. Pure, clean water is best for flowers. Some of the elements in tap water can be harmful for flowers—for example, too much fluoride or iron. A water purifier attached to your tap will help.

9. Mild soap and bleach are needed to clean flower containers thoroughly. A drop of bleach with mild soap cleans any residue and kills bacteria that might inhibit the life of flowers. Premix the bleach, soap, and water in a large spray bottle, and keep on hand.

10. Twine and threads in shades of browns and greens are used for several purposes. See care and conditioning tips 17 and 29 and arranging tip 17.

11. A meat baster or a thin spouted watering can is useful to keep containers filled and stems in deep water. These choices make it easy to fill containers that hold several stems or branches.

12. Gloves keep hands protected from stains or the harmful secretions of certain flowers. Medical gloves work well, since they are thin and tight-fitting and don't interfere with the handling of the flowers.

13. A mister is used to cool flowers temporarily while providing an extra source of water and moisture.

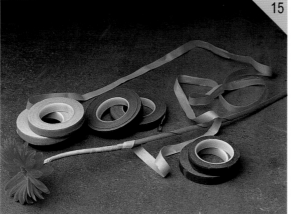

14. Floral wire is used for many purposes, such as repairing and straightening flowers. See care and conditioning tip 31 and arranging tips 18 and 20.

15. Floral tape and regular heavy-duty tape, such as duct tape, are useful. See care and conditioning tip 31e and arranging tip 19.

16. An assortment of plastic or glass containers in various sizes is needed for proper hydration of the flowers.

17. Straight branches or sticks such as bamboo or willow branches aid in supporting heavy flowers for proper hydration. See care and conditioning tip 29 and arranging tip 17.

18. Heavy paper, such as newspaper or butcher's paper, aids in straightening and supporting certain flowers. See care and conditioning tip 35.

Opposite. For decorative purposes, just about any container will work for flowers, from an old antique paint can to the most elegant crystal vase. The choice of container influences the appearance of flowers.

1. Do not place flowers directly into containers that are metal, rusted, or made of clay or stone. These materials are porous, and may contain elements that are harmful to flowers. It is best to line your container with glass or plastic. Glass and plastic are the best materials to contain flowers.

2. Containers should be clean and sterile before being filled with water and flowers. Clean, sterile containers are essential to the vase life of the flowers.

3. Containers should be as deep as possible, considering the length of the flower stem. Flowers last longer in deep water.

handling flowers

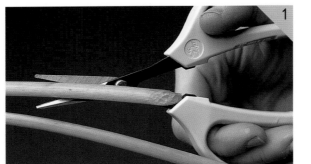

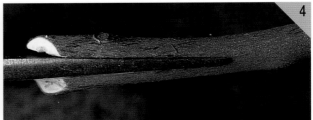

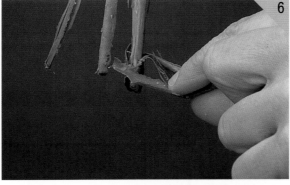

1. Always cut stems at a sharp angle. This increases the surface area of the stem and allows water to be better absorbed through the stem.

2. Stems cut at an angle will not rest flush against the bottom of the container; thus they allow the water to penetrate the stem.

3. After the end of the stem is cut, place it directly into the water. It only takes a minute for the stem to begin to dry and seal up.

4. Thick stems and thin branches should be cut at an angle, and then cut up the center for better water absorption through the fibrous stems.

5. Hammer all thick, woody stems and branches about five to six inches up from the bottom, and make several splits in the stem. This allows for better water absorption.

6. Remove the extra bark around the shattered part of the stem to prevent contaminating the water. This will prolong the vase life of the flowers.

7. Pull or trim all leaves and thorns that will be below the water level in the container. Allowing such materials to decompose in water will allow harmful bacteria to shorten the life of the flowers.

8. Scrape all of the small debris on the stem—such as small thorns, branching stems, etc.—with a sharp, curved knife to thoroughly clean the stem before it is placed in the water.

9. Clean stems should be placed in the deepest water possible to promote vase life. Water can be absorbed from the outside part of the stem as well as the base. A nick or crack in the stem left exposed above the water level can create an air pocket and block water flow to the flower. The deeper the water, the less likely this is to occur.

10. In conditioning flowers, the water temperature should be comfortably warm. Submerge your hand to test the water. Cold water is not as readily absorbed by the flower. Hot water will penetrate the stem, but will almost shock the flower.

11. Once flowers are placed in water, they begin to decompose or break down by releasing gases and forming bacteria. The cleaner the stems and the less debris in the water, the less decomposition occurs, and the longer the flowers will last.

12. All the same kind of flower in a vase or container will last longer than a mix of different types. Certain flowers have a different makeup and decompose by different means. This mixed reaction can shorten the life of all the flowers. The same kind of flower will break down by the same reaction. Actually, a single flower in a vase will last longer than several of the same kind.

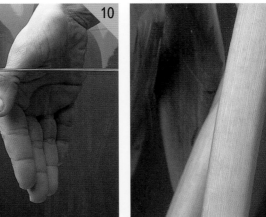

13. Cloudy or discolored water is an indication of decomposition and bacterial growth. Change the water in the container at least every couple of days, using new, warm water. This will open the stems to allow water to flow to the flower.

14. Fresh, clean water is best for the vase life of flowers. Some commercial floral foods can lengthen the vase life as well, but be very careful in measuring the amount. Using too much can actually be harmful. Homemade versions or substitutions, such as lemon lime soda, are not a good idea, because sugar promotes bacterial growth in the water.

15. Stems will develop a film and become discolored from stagnating in the water; this blocks water flow to the flower. Recut the stems each time the water is changed to allow water to penetrate the stem.

16. Mixed arrangements are sometimes hard to disassemble to change the water and to recut the stems. Flushing the container with fresh water will help somewhat to prolong the life of the bouquet. Use the tap or the spray nozzle on your sink full force for a few minutes with warm water to flush the container completely.

17a, b, c. Use a piece of heavy twine to tie your arrangement at the top of the container. Once the flowers are tied snugly, pull them from the vase. Clean the vase, and change the water. Hold the tied bouquet upside down. Recut all the stems at an angle. Place back into the container and cut the twine. Your bouquet should fall back into place.

23. Purchased cut flowers will usually be wrapped in paper or cellophane to protect them. It is a good idea to leave them wrapped and hydrating in deep water for about an hour when they are brought home before conditioning or arranging them. This will ensure the flowers will be upright.

24. Pinching or trimming off spent blossoms and leaves encourages other blossoms to open and makes the flower last longer. The spent blossoms take some of the energy the flower has to stay alive. Trimming these away allows the flower to channel the energy to the healthy parts.

25. Some flowers, such as carnations and dahlias, have separations or nodes along their stems. The stem is thicker and more fibrous at these parts. Cut the stem between the nodes to allow water to penetrate the stem.

26. Branching or spray flowers will last longer if the stems are separated at their base. This allows for water to be directly absorbed by each blossom.

27a

27b

27a, b. Some flowers secrete sap or latex when cut. Singeing the ends will keep this fluid contained in the stem. The fluid is what the flower needs to last. Some believe that placing the end in boiling water will seal the stem. This works, but the hot steam is not good for the flower itself; burning the end works the best. Try using a gas flame on a stove, or a candle with an extra-thick wick. Singe about one-half to one inch of the base of the stem.

28. Poisonous flowers are best used alone in their own container. These flowers secrete latex that is harmful to other flowers. Condition by standing them in deep water with a drop of bleach for 24 hours before mixing with other flowers.

29. Tall or heavy flowers, such as lilies and hybrid delphiniums, may bend or break before they are completely hydrated. Tie the tip of the flower and the middle part of the stem to a branch or stick loosely with twine to support the flower for proper hydration.

30a. Flowers with hollow stems, such as amaryllis, are designed to draw water up through the outer layers of the stem. Some believe that filling the stem with water and plugging the end will help the flower last longer. This may help, but it is unnecessary because of the way the flower is designed.

30b. Hollow stems will crack and break more easily than solid stems. Support them by slowly inserting a stick into the end of the flower. A clean branch or bamboo works well. Covering the stick with a soft, water-absorbent material will protect the inside of the stem and provide extra moisture as well.

28

29

30a

30b

31a

31b

31c

31d

31a. Bent or cracked stems and flowers that bend owing to their heavy heads can be salvaged with floral wire. Insert the wire partway into the strong area above the bend or break, or under the flower head. Also see arranging tip 18.

31b. Support the stem with the wire and straighten it to the upright position.

31c. Gently wrap the wire around the rest of the stem.

31d. Wrap the stem or the point of incision with floral tape to keep air from blocking water to the stem.

32. If flowers wilt or droop prematurely, cutting them short and placing them in slightly warmer water should revive them. Both the cutting and water temperature help the blossom absorb water more quickly.

33. Some flowers bend or droop because their flower heads become too heavy for their stems. The stems become water-logged and stop conveying water to the blossom. A tiny prick just below the head of the flower will release air, thus increasing the water flow.

34. Wilted flowers can also be revived by completely submerging them in cool water. Do this by filling a deep bucket or tub with cool water. Place the flowers lying down in the water and weigh them down with a weight of some kind, like a brick. Let the flowers stay submerged for a few hours.

35a

35a. Some flowers bend or droop owing to light, temperature changes, or just because it is the nature of that flower.

35b. To straighten flowers, place them one by one on a damp paper, lining them up evenly .

35c. Gently roll the paper around the flowers, forming a cone shape.

35d. Secure the paper with twine or with staples so that the paper braces the flowers.

35e (opposite). Mist the flowers and paper to keep them damp. Place the cone of flowers in deep water for several hours.

35f. Unwrap the flowers and they will be upright again.

35f

35b

35c

35d

1 (opposite). The best way to arrange flowers is to appreciate them in their natural state. If the flower is tall, opens, leans, etc., arrange it to suit that characteristic. Even if the flower is manipulated somewhat to fit into a certain type of arrangement, it is still best to utilize it according to its character. Let vines drape around the base of arrangements, leave room for flowers to open and close, etc.

2. The best way to start an arrangement is by making a good base. Many believe in using arranging devices such as floral foam, frogs, chicken wire, etc. These items are quite useful, but may create an almost unnatural bouquet as well as shortening the vase life of the flowers.

3. Floral foam is very useful in flower arranging, because it holds each flower in place. However, when stems are inserted into foam, the foam covers and clogs the ends. The flowers will not last as long as when they are arranged in water.

4. Arranging frogs have a similar effect on flowers. The end of the stem is partially blocked by the prongs inserted into the stem, inhibiting water flow to the flower.

5a. Chicken wire wedged into the container adds a metal material to the water that may react to the flowers. It can also damage stems as they are being placed into the container, thus further contaminating the water.

5b. Chicken wire secured around the top of the container is a better method.

6. A more natural way of starting an arrangement is to create a base with full, thick foliage. This base will help secure flowers in place when building an arrangement. Pick foliage that is similar to the flower choices for the most natural look.

7. When creating a base for an arrangement with foliage or flowers, place a few stems into the container and turn the container. Repeat this a few times to create a maze of intertwining stems. This will hold the other flowers and material in place to build the arrangement.

8. When flowers are cut shorter to use in bouquets, the best "filler," or greenery, is the flowers' own foliage. Save the excess that is cut off for use in and around the flowers.

9. When arranging in a vase that is too large for the number of flowers being used, fill the vase with the base of a branch. The branch acts as a natural maze for the flowers to brace against. The flowers stay in place as you build the arrangement, enabling you to use fewer of them.

10. Flowers with large, curved leaves, such as tulips, can be useful in arranging because leaving the leaf intact can act as a brace for the flower, and a few can make a nice base for other flowers to be added.

11. Leaving the thorns on stems is another way to create a natural base for a flower arrangement. The thorns will hold the stems together, so other flowers added will also be held in place.

12. Tying a grouping of flowers like snap-dragons or carnations together with thread or twine can create a nice base for arrangements. This method can also be used in securing taller stems of the same type of flower when building an arrange-ment. This is much easier than securing individual stems.

13. Tall flowers can be cut short and short flowers can be lengthened to suit the arrangement. See arranging tip 20.

14. Use large-blossomed flowers such as hydrangeas or amaryllis cut down for the base of an arrangement. The blossoms fill the vase opening, allowing the other flowers to be secured among and around them.

15. Tall flowers with several graduating blossoms, such as gladiolas and snapdragons, can be cut at the tips to encourage the other blossoms to open more quickly. This does alter the natural appearance of the flower, but it is helpful in speeding the blooming process.

16. Tightly budded flowers can be added to arrangements for interesting texture and a natural look. Place them among the fully blossomed flowers.

17. Some flowers continue to grow and develop in water after they are cut. These flowers are sometimes difficult to arrange, because they change daily. Use thin green thread or twine to tie them to a branch or sturdy flower in the arrangement, which helps keep them in place and tidy.

18a. Floral wires are useful in securing flowers or bending a flower a certain way to make it fit better into an arrangement. Place the wire just under the head. Insert the wire about one-eighth to one-quarter inch into the flower.

18b. Straighten the flower to an upright position, or bend the flower into the desired position.

18c. Gently fold the wire closely around the bottom part of the stem. The stem is now secured or can be maneuvered.

19. Wrapping floral tape similar in color to the stem around the length of the stem will hide the wire and aid in preventing an air pocket. See care and conditioning tip 31e.

20a. Floral wires are useful in lengthening the stems of flowers with short stems, or flowers that have been cut too short for an arrangement. Simply place the wire in the bottom of the stem about two inches, and cut the wire the desired length.

20b. The wire end will act as the stem end resting in the container.

21(opposite). There is a "rule" that an arrangement should be one and one-half times the height of the container. However, this rule does not necessarily apply. Flower stems summered in a vase with just their heads peeking over the rim can be just as attractive as a proportioned bouquet.

22. The most elaborate combination or the simplest of bouquets can be transformed by the container choice. Pick a container to enhance the flowers. This bright blue container displays the flowers in a more interesting way than would a plain glass vase.

1. When planting, start with a good soil mix. Make sure it is light and airy, and rich in nutrients. If the soil is clayey or heavy, it may retain too much moisture or suffocate the plant. This is true whether you are planting in containers, forcing bulbs, or preparing your garden beds.

2. Most flowering plants and bulbs need proper watering to thrive. Too much water or too little can be harmful. Discoloration of leaves is an indication of a watering problem. If you can squeeze water from a handful of soil, then the plant has too much water. Water your plants gently, allowing them to drink slowly and being careful not to drench them all at once, which may give them a shock.

3. Some plants and bulbs prefer to be watered from beneath, so that they can absorb the amount they need slowly and hydrate as they wish.

4. Be careful not to leave container plants sitting in stagnant water that drains from a watering. Stagnant water causes plants to become too moist. Placing a few rocks or pebbles in the saucer allows excess water to drain.

5. Most flowering plants benefit from misting with cool water. The cooler temperature aids exterior water absorption and refreshes the plant.

6. Water plants and flowers in the garden when the sun is low, either morning or evening. Do not water them in the heat of the day, when water on the flowers and leaves may scorch the plant.

7. Proper fertilization is helpful. Nutrients are important to a plant's development, but be careful not to overfertilize: More is not always better. Read instructions carefully and follow the guidelines. Too much fertilizer actually harms plants, inhibiting instead of promoting growth.

8. Cut flowers in the morning or evening. Flowers cut at midday may not hold up.

9. Flowers from the garden are the best source for cutting. However, when your garden is not producing in abundance, buy plants from nurseries, greenhouses, florists and grocery stores. The flowers are still growing and can be kept until they are used. Cut what you need to use and allow the plant to produce more flowers.

10a. When forcing bulbs to bloom in winter, plant them shoulder to shoulder and leave the top one-third to one-half of the bulb exposed to prevent rot. Close planting and partial exposure cut down on excess moisture and allow a greater show of flowers.

10b. Gently scrape away the dry roots on the bottom of the bulb. It will root more quickly and be less likely to rot.

11a. Place rocks or broken terra-cotta pieces in the bottom of the container before planting to help with drainage.

11b. Mixing a little sand and horticultural charcoal into the soil mixture also helps drainage and keeps the soil fresh.

12. When planting bulbs outside, they should generally be planted at a depth of two and one-half times their diameter. Bulbs planted too deep or too shallow will not perform as well.

13. Make sure bulbs and plants are not crowded when planted—the roots need room to grow if the plant is to flourish.

14. Cutting back garden plants after their flowering period or to produce more flowers should follow one rule: Only cut back what is dry and discolored. While a plant is green, it is still in its cycle, and cutting back too soon can actually inhibit growth for the next year.

15. Multiflowering plants should be trimmed back as the blossoms are spent to encourage more blooms to develop.

16. Some plants, such as delphinium, can be fooled into blooming a second time. Once a flower has bloomed, cut the entire plant back to the ground, leaving only the base of foliage. The plant will actually force itself to produce a second flower. It may lack some of the height and bloom count of the first, but for the most part will produce a second beautiful flower.

17. Some plants can be forced to become larger. When the plant sends up its initial flower stalk, cut the stalk back to the base of the leaves. The plant will then send up multiple shoots, producing more flowers.

18. To produce a large flower from a plant that usually produces several blossoms, focus on one bud, trimming the others away so the plant can focus its energy. This method is known as "disbudding."

19. Plants should be divided every few years to give them a vigorous new start and make them stronger bloomers. Wash away the soil from the roots before you make the division, so that you can see the best place to cut or pull. Be sure to leave a good clump of roots for each section.

20. When growing plants from seeds, make sure not to crowd them, as this will inhibit growth. If seedlings appear crowded, pull the smallest and weakest, concentrating on the healthy ones.

21. Protect your garden with nutrient-rich mulch over the winter, concentrating on the most frost-sensitive plants that need extra protection to survive. Plant according to your temperature zone if you want plants to return and thrive every year. Some perennials can be planted as annuals in cooler climates.

flowers A to Z

1. Agapanthus are tall, with round clusters of lily-shaped flowers atop thick, dark-green stems. The stem is usually one to three feet in length. A fresh agapanthus has one-third of its blossoms opening, with the rest in bud stage. The blossoms turn upward. If you shake the flower gently, the blossoms will not drop.

2. Older agapanthus have dropped some flowers—the small bare stems within the flower clusters indicate this. Some of the blossoms may also be dried out or discolored. The flowers drop more profusely with age, and appear to turn downward.

3. When the flowers drop, keep the small, bare stems cut back at the base of the cluster to help the other blossoms open. Stems and spent blossoms that are not cut back inhibit the others from opening. See care and conditioning tip 24. This extra care lengthens the vase life of the flowers.

4. Agapanthus cut very short, two to three inches below the base of the cluster, are tucked into this bouquet so that just the flowers are revealed. This gives an exotic flower a sweeter, more old-fashioned appearance.

NAMES: Agapanthus, African Lily, Lily of the Nile.
COLORS: Shades of light blue to deep purple-blue, and the more uncommon white.
SCENT: None.
FRESHNESS: About one-third of the blossoms are opening, with the open blossoms slightly turned upward. The flowers and buds do not drop when handled. (However, some of the open flowers will drop before other blossoms open.)
VASE LIFE: 7 to 10 days, or longer.
AVAILABILITY: All year, but the predominant season is summer. Bulbs are available late winter to early spring.
COST: Moderately expensive.
MEANING: Agapanthus means "love flower" in Greek.
ARRANGING TIP: These exotic flowers make such a statement that just a few stems are impressive alone. Agapanthus can also be cut very short and used in mixed arrangements, taking on a more old-fashioned appearance.
GROWING TIP: This flower can be grown indoors much like the amaryllis, but blooms in the summer. See planting instructions for amaryllis on page 54.

1. Alliums are clusters of small, star-shaped blossoms. a) The blossoms can be compact, forming a round, globelike cluster such as that seen in the popular giganteum variety on the left. This variety can reach four to six feet in height. b) Alliums can also be small, loose sprays of blossoms.

2. A fresh allium should have one-third to one-half of its blossoms open.

3. Older allium flowers have most of their blossoms open, with some dried out. The onion odor may be more noticeable.

4. The small white spray known as *Allium neapolitanum* is the only variety with a sweet, pleasant scent. This variety makes an excellent cut flower for arrangements.

NAMES: Allium, Ornamental Onion Flower.
VARIETIES: There are over 400 varieties of alliums. Alliums are composed of many star-shaped blossoms, which may be compact to form a round cluster, or loose sprays of blossoms. See photos 1a and 1b.
COLORS: Most alliums come in shades of purple, but some varieties are available in white, pink, or yellow.
SCENT: Slight onion scent, becoming noticeable when the flowers are bruised, damaged, or aging.
FRESHNESS: Alliums should have one-third to one-half of their blossoms open.
VASE LIFE: 10 days up to 3 weeks. Change the water frequently to prevent odor from developing.
AVAILABILITY: Late spring through summer.
COST: The giganteum variety—expensive. Other varieties—inexpensive to moderately priced.
MEANING: European folklore ascribed magical properties to the ornamental onion. The plant was used for good luck and protection against demons.
ARRANGING TIP: Be very careful not to bruise the flowers when arranging, as this will release the onion odor. See arranging tip 13.
GROWING TIP: Alliums are very easy to grow, multiplying rapidly. They do well in poor or dry soil, and in full sun or shade. The flowers can last up to a month in the garden. Plant the tall, big-blossomed varieties in an area protected from wind, since the stems break easily. See growing tip 12.
OTHER: See care and conditioning tips 24 and 35.

1. Amaryllis or Hippeastrum are tall flowers having thick green stems with two to five large, trumpet-shaped blossoms at the top. Mini amaryllis are basically the same flower, but much shorter and with smaller blossoms.

2. Amaryllis Belladonna has pink blossoms and deep brown stems. This variety is fragrant.

3. A fresh amaryllis has most of its blossoms closed, or just one beginning to open. The buds show good color and size, and the stem feels strong and sturdy. It is normal for the bottom of the stem to curl. This is not an indication of freshness.

4. Older amaryllis have most of their flowers open, with the tips beginning to dry out or becoming discolored. The stems feel weak, and older ones may start to crack or break.

5. Mostly used in tall bouquets, amaryllis cut down with a few other flowers make a full, impressive, long-lasting arrangement that does not require a lot of flowers.

NAMES: Amaryllis or Hippeastrum, Amaryllis Belladonna or Belladonna Lily.

VARIETIES: The true Amaryllis Belladonna variety is seen in photo 2, and the Hippeastrum hybrids, which are the more common amaryllis, are pictured in photo 1. Hippeastrums are available in single and double varieties as well.

COLORS: White, pale yellow or green; shades of pink; salmon, red, and burgundy. Some are striped or variegated.

SCENT: None, except for the Belladonna variety, which has a mild, sweet fragrance.

FRESHNESS: Most of the blossoms are closed, but show good color and size. Watch for bruises on the tips of the blossoms.

VASE LIFE: Approximately 7 to 10 days or longer.

AVAILABILITY: Amaryllis Hippeastrum is available December to April for cut flowers. The bulbs are available in the fall. The Belladonna variety is available in late August to early October.

COST: Winter—expensive. Spring—moderately expensive.

MEANING: This dramatic flower symbolizes pride.

ARRANGING TIP: Amaryllis stand about 24 inches or more. They make an impressive statement alone or mixed in tall arrangements, but can be just as showy cut down for shorter bouquets. See arranging tip 14.

GROWING TIP: To force amaryllis bulbs, pick a container only slightly larger than the bulb. Amaryllis bulbs like to be crowded, because they rot easily and a smaller space cuts down on excess moisture. Plant the bulb with one-third of its surface exposed. Water once and place in medium to strong light. Do not water again until there is a sign of growth. Then water once or twice a week. When the bulb is finished flowering, continue watering until the stalk and leaves die back, thus nourishing the bulb for the next flowering. Stop watering, place in a cool, dark spot for approximately six months, then start the process again. The older the bulb, the more flower stalks the bulb will produce. Purchasing older or aged bulbs is well worth the cost and effort. See growing tip 11.

OTHER: Amaryllis in bud stage opens slowly and turns toward the light. Make sure this flower is in an evenly lit place, or you may need to turn the vase or pot to ensure a well-developed blossom. See care and conditioning tip 30.

1. Anemones are cup-shaped flowers in rich jewel colors. The centers are pale green or black. A fresh anemone has a tight, clean center without pollen developing. The petals show good color and are close together.

2. Older anemones have pollinated centers. The petals are slightly faded in color and have become separated more from one another.

3. Anemones will open in the light and in a heated environment, and close in the dark or in cooler temperatures. They will also curve or bend toward the light. Keep them in medium light and in a cooler spot to prolong life. Remember this also when arranging with anemones. See care and conditioning tip 18.

4. The Japanese anemone is similar to the florist anemones seen in the other photos, but has smaller flowers and is available in shades of white and pink. This variety is the best choice for the garden, blooming in late summer to first frost. It also makes a good cut flower. *Anemone coronaria* or the florist anemone, is not very hardy and has a short growing season, from about late April to mid-May.

NAMES: Anemone, Windflower.

VARIETIES: *A. coronaria* are the traditional florist anemones. Single, double, and semidouble varieties are available. Anemone De Caen and Mona Lisa varieties, which are much taller and with larger flowers, were developed from this variety.

COLORS: White, shades of pink and purple, magenta, and burgundy. The middles can be pale green or black.

SCENT: None.

FRESHNESS: The flowers have clean, tight centers with no pollination. The petals have good, solid color, and are close together, forming a cup shape.

VASE LIFE: 5 to 7 days. Keep anemones in medium light and in a cool spot to prolong vase life.

AVAILABILITY: Available as a cut flower December to May, but the season is primarily spring.

COST: Winter—moderately expensive. Spring—moderately priced.

MEANING: To forsake.

NOTE: Anemones are the flowers referred to as "the lilies of the field" in the Old Testament.

ARRANGING TIP: Anemones will open in light and heat, so leave room in your arrangements for them to do so or they may crowd other flowers and give an unnatural appearance to the bouquet.

GROWING TIP: Japanese anemones are a hardier variety, with a longer blooming season. This is the best choice for the garden, and makes good cut flowers. Japanese anemones are available in whites and pinks.

OTHER: Anemones are heavy drinkers, so check the water level frequently.

1. Bouvardia are clusters of small tubular flowers with four equal petals atop slender woody stems. A fresh bouvardia should be mostly in bud stage, with only one to two flowers open. The buds should show good color.

2. Older bouvardia have most of their flowers open; some may have started to bend or drop from the cluster. Bouvardia bruise very easily when handled.

3. Bouvardia are prone to premature wilting because water has difficulty penetrating the dense woody stems to reach the branching flower clusters. To prolong vase life, recut the stems and place into deep, fresh warm water frequently. This will help keep a steady water flow to the flowers. Also, tear off any excess greenery and blossoms so that more water reaches the primary blossoms.

NAMES: Bouvardia.
VARIETIES: Bouvardian hybrids in single and double varieties.
COLORS: Whites, pinks, peaches, red, and a new green shade.
SCENT: Very faint to none.
FRESHNESS: The buds show color, and only a couple of blossoms are open. The flowers bruise very easily.
VASE LIFE: Approximately 5 days. Bouvardia are very water sensitive. There is a special floral food available at most florists for Bouvardia, which aids in water absorption.
AVAILABILITY: All year, but summer and fall are the predominant seasons.
COST: Moderately priced.
ARRANGING TIP: Bouvardia are a popular choice for a wedding bouquet flower, but remember that they do not hold up out of water.
OTHER: See care and conditioning tips 4, 24, and 32.

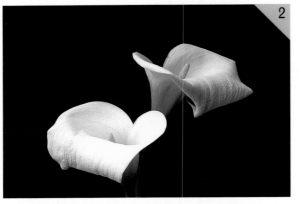

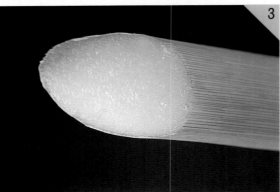

1. Calla lilies are exquisite flowers with long trumpet-shaped blossoms and thick fibrous stems. A fresh calla is mostly open, but with the outer petal still reaching upward. The middle of the flower is clean, with no signs of pollination. The flower shows good color with no bruising.

2. Older callas have the outer petal curving downward, with the middle of the flower exposed. The middle shows signs of pollen. The flowers may also have bruising or discoloration, especially on the outer edges of the petal.

3. Callas have thick, fibrous stems that act much like a sponge. The stems absorb and hold water. This is why callas have such a long vase life. They are a very low-maintenance flower, but be sure to recut the stems every few days to allow fresh water to penetrate to the blossom. Calla stems sometimes turn to mush because the stems hold the water and the ends become clogged. They need a constant water flow to remain fresh.

4. Flame-colored calla lilies in a vase are elegant in their simplicity.

NAMES: Calla Lily, Arum Lily, Zantedeschia.
VARIETIES: The most common is the tall white variety, two to three feet in length. Zantedeschias are also available in miniature varieties.
COLORS: White, shades of yellow, pink to deep rose, orange to Chinese red, salmon, burgundy, black. There is also a green variety called "green goddess."
SCENT: None.
SCENT: The flowers are open, but the outer petal (or spathe) still turns upward. The middle is clean and shows no pollination. Watch for bruising.
VASE LIFE: 10 days or more. Callas are designed to hold water.
AVAILABILITY: All year, but late winter to late spring is the peak season.
COST: Expensive.
MEANING: Calla lilies symbolize magnificent beauty.
NOTE: The white calla has long been a symbol of purity, and is widely used in weddings as well as funerals.
ARRANGING TIP: The calla lily is the epitome of elegance. These flowers can add drama to any combination, but have just as strong a presence used alone.
OTHER: Check the water level frequently, since calla lilies are heavy drinkers. See also care and conditioning tip 35.

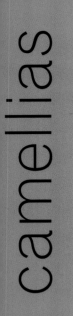

1. Camellias should be cut or bought when the buds show good size and color. The buds should be starting to crack open. This will ensure that the buds develop and blossom fully.

2. Full camellia blossoms fall off the branches easily. The blossoms also bruise when handled.

3. The best way to enjoy camellia flowers is to float them in a container. Buds will also open and develop with this method.

4. Camellias are mostly used for their shiny, dark-green leaves, which pair well with flowers lacking good foliage of their own. Camellia leaves are paired with miniature carnations. The dark-green of the camellia leaves accents the flowers better than does their own foliage.

NAMES: Camellia.
VARIETIES: There are some 82 species of camellias. The common camellia, grown for its beautiful waxlike flowers, is the *Camellia japonica*. There are single and double varieties available.
COLORS: Whites, creams, pinks, and reds. Solid and variegated shades.
SCENT: Very mild sweet fragrance.
FRESHNESS: Buds are good size and show color.
VASE LIFE: Greenery lasts for weeks, the blossoms only a few days. Flowers drop from their branches easily.
AVAILABILITY: Greenery available all year. The blossoms appear in the late winter/early spring and again in the fall.
COST: Inexpensive.
MEANING: The flower of graciousness. The red camellia is for loveliness.
NOTE: The tea that we drink is made from a variety of camellia.
ARRANGING TIP: Float camellia blossoms in a bowl to enjoy the flowers. Camellia foliage is useful when arranging with most types of flowers. See arranging tips 6 and 16.
OTHER: See care and conditioning tips 5, 6, and 24.

1. Carnations are large single or miniature multistemmed flowers with compact blossoms made up of many frilled petals. They are sometimes referred to as "pinks," because the edges of the petals appear to be cut with pinking shears.

2. A fresh carnation should be about half open, and the miniature spray variety should have a few flowers half to fully open, with the others in bud.

3. Older carnations will be fully open, with some of the dense petals curving outward. The edges of the petals may have started to discolor and dry out.

4. This variety of dianthus is called sweet william. It is available in the spring and early summer in shades of red, pink, and white. Sweet william is a long-lasting cut flower as well as a popular garden flower.

5. Large pink carnations cut down and massed together almost resemble garden roses or peonies.

NAMES: Carnation, Dianthus.
VARIETIES: There are over 300 species of dianthus, and hundreds of varieties. The common florist carnations or English carnation is available in large single blooms and in a miniature or spray variety with five to six flowers per stem.
COLORS: Available in an enormous array of shades and colors; some varieties are bicolored or variegated. The most common colors are red, pink, white, and burgundy. Carnations are a popular flower to dye.
SCENT: Some have a fresh clove scent.
FRESHNESS: The flowers are about half open. The spray variety has a few flowers half to fully open, with the rest in bud.
VASE LIFE: 10 days to 2 weeks, sometimes longer. Although this is a long-lasting flower, be careful when handling carnations, as their heads can pop off easily.
AVAILABILITY: All year.
COST: Inexpensive.
MEANING: A pink carnation is the symbol of mother's love and the emblem of Mother's Day. Other colors have their own meanings: Yellow is for disdain, purple for antipathy, striped for refusal. White is for pure and ardent love, while red means "Alas my poor heart."
ARRANGING TIP: Carnations are inexpensive, very long-lasting flowers, so one would expect them to be a favorite. However, they are shunned by many as cheap and undesirable. Carnations can be manipulated to take on an elegant look by massing them together in a tight bunch, as in photo 5, or adding them to simple greenery (see photo 4 on page 64). They are also an inexpensive choice to fill in or to cover parts of arrangements. See also arranging tip 12.
OTHER: See care and conditioning tips 25 and 26.

1. Chrysanthemums come in a huge variety of shapes and sizes. They are separated into 13 categories, depending on the blossom type or shape of the petals. Chrysanthemums can be single blossoms or sprays with several flowers. The blossoms range from daisy to cushion or button types. They can be single or have double layers of petals. The petals can curve inward, called incurve, or be reflexed, curving out.

2. A popular type of chrysanthemum, especially in autumn to wear to football games, is the very large round blossom type with incurve petals. This variety has been nicknamed football mums.

3. Chrysanthemums are a very long-lasting flower. It is best to purchase or cut them when the flowers are fully open. Cut too early in bud stage, they will not open. The daisy types will have the middle exposed. Other types, such as the cushion or button blossoms, will be open, but the middle will appear to have petals to open further. Fresh chrysanthemums show good color and are firm to the touch.

4. Older chrysanthemums have petals faded in color. The petals may become more separated with age, and the flower may feel almost soft to the touch. It may shed some of its petals when handled.

5. The common daisy belongs to the chrysanthemum family.

NAMES: Chrysanthemum, Mum.
VARIETIES: About 1,000 different varieties.
COLORS: Available in most shades but no true blue. Some are two-toned and multicolored.
SCENT: A strong musk scent.
FRESHNESS: Purchase or cut when the flowers are three-fourths to fully open. Flowers in bud will usually not open after being cut.
VASE LIFE: 10 days to 2 weeks or longer.
AVAILABILITY: All year, but the prime season is summer.
COST: Inexpensive.
MEANING: The name *chrysanthemum* means "golden flower" in Greek. Individual colors have their own meanings: Red symbolizes love, white symbolizes truth, yellow symbolizes slighted love. Snubbed in some countries as a funeral flower, the chrysanthemum is the national symbol of Japan, where it signifies long life and happiness.
ARRANGING TIP: Chrysanthemums are a very long-lasting cut flower and popular for use in arrangements. But they can shorten the vase life of other flowers and are best used alone. See below.
OTHER: Chrysanthemums have thick, coarse stems which one would normally hammer or split. However, these flowers should be cut at a diagonal instead, owing to the large amounts of gas they give off. Change the water frequently to avoid an overabundance of harmful bacteria. A few pieces of horticultural charcoal in the water will help absorb some of the bacteria between water changes. See care and conditioning tip 26.

COSMOS

1. Cosmos resemble daisies, with a single or double row of petals surrounding their centers. The blossoms are surrounded by delicate, lacy foliage. Cosmos can grow from a foot to as much as six feet in height. A fresh cosmos will have just started to open. The petals will still be turned upward, and there will be little or no signs of pollination in the center of the flower.

2. Older cosmos have petals turning downward, and the centers show signs of pollen formation. The petals feel soft to the touch.

3. The unusual chocolate cosmos is deep burgundy brown in color, with a velvety texture. The flower does smell like chocolate.

4. Just adding a few cosmos to any combination can create the perfect casual summer bouquet.

NAMES: Cosmos.
VARIETIES: The most common variety and the best for cut flowers is *Cosmos bipinnatus.* Single and double varieties are available, as well as the more unusual variety known as chocolate cosmos or *Cosmos atrosanguineus.*
COLORS: Mostly shades of pink, salmon, red, and white, with some candy-stripe shades.
SCENT: None, except for the chocolate variety.
FRESHNESS: Purchase or cut when the flowers have just started to open but the petals are not completely lying flat. The buds will also open after they are cut.
VASE LIFE: 3 to 5 days. When cosmos are cut from the source, they can last 10 days or longer.
AVAILABILITY: The middle of summer to fall.
COST: Inexpensive. The chocolate variety—moderately priced.
MEANING: Cosmos comes from the Greek word for order and harmony.
ARRANGING TIP: These beautiful, airy flowers are perfect for casual summer bouquets.
GROWING TIP: Few plants grow as rapidly as cosmos. Seeds can be sown directly into the soil after the danger of frost is over, and will produce many blossoms from midsummer to the first frost. They do best when cut from the source. The shorter variety called Sonata can easily be grown in containers as well. See growing tip 20.
NOTE: Cosmos attract butterflies to the garden.
OTHER: See care and conditioning tips 24 and 26.

1. Cyclamen have colorful, sharp reflexed petals atop deep-brown stems. The leaves are heart shaped and a deep marble green color. This flower is mostly sold as a potted plant blooming in the fall and winter months.

2. Cyclamen plants prefer to be watered from beneath. Water as needed, being careful not to overwater, as the root rots easily. The leaves will seem droopy and be soft to the touch when they need a drink. Water just enough to keep the soil damp.

3. Plants must be properly trimmed back to encourage new growth. Trim the spent flowers and any yellow leaves at their base.

4. Cyclamen flowers resemble butterflies on top of this spring bouquet.

NAMES: Cyclamen.
VARIETIES: There are about 20 species. The common or florist ones are the *Cyclamen persicum* varieties. These are available in large flowering types and miniature varieties.
COLORS: White, red, pink, and violet shades.
SCENT: None.
FRESHNESS: Plants have only a few flowers fully open, with several in bud stage. At the base of the plant, more young buds are sprouting. The leaves are firm and dark, marble green in color, with no brown spots.
VASE LIFE: Cut flowers will last 7 to 10 days or longer. Plants properly cared for will last for months and keep producing flowers.
AVAILABILITY: Plants are available from fall to late spring.
COST: Moderately priced.
MEANING: Diffidence or shyness.
ARRANGING TIP: Cyclamen flowers take on a new look when clipped away from their heart-shaped leaves. Try single stems for a stark look, or add flowers to the top of a bouquet for a different effect.
GROWING TIP: Cyclamen plants need to be watered from beneath. Allow the plant to drink slowly, absorbing as much water as needed. Watering from above may damage the tuber or root of the plant. Do not let the plants rest in water for an extended time, as plants can easily rot this way as well. Cyclamen prefer bright but indirect light, as well as a cool spot in the house. Keep spent flowers and leaves clipped back at the base to encourage new sprouts. See growing tips 2, 3, and 4.
OTHER: See care and conditioning tip 24.

1. Daffodils come in many varieties. They may have single or multiple blooms, large or small cups, split or double middles, flat or reflexed petals. They come in solid colors and a variety of combinations.

2. Daffodils should be cut or purchased in bud stage. The bud should show good color, but a little green is fine. The buds open very quickly.

3. Older daffodils start to wrinkle and fade in color. Check closely for this when buying.

4. A popular type called paper-white narcissus is primarily used at Christmas time. The most common variety is called Ziva, which has a very strong fragrance. An almost identical variety called Galilee has a milder fragrance and does not grow as tall.

5. When picking daffodils, do not cut, but pinch the stems at the base with your fingers. This partially closes the stem and somewhat inhibits the latex serum in the stem from contaminating the water. The blooms will then last longer and can be mixed with other flowers in bouquets. Do not pick the leaves—this is the bulbs' nourishment for the next season.

NAMES: Daffodil, Narcissus (the formal name is narcissus).
VARIETIES: There are thousands of varieties of daffodils, separated into 11 different divisions depending on blossom type. See photo 1.
COLORS: The large yellow daffodil is the most common and popular. Varieties come in all shades of yellow and white, but some have green, orange, apricot, pink, or crimson coloring.
SCENT: Most varieties have a clean, sweet scent, but some, such as the paper-white narcissus Ziva, can be almost overpowering.
FRESHNESS: All varieties should be cut or purchased in bud stage. The spray varieties may have one or two blossoms opening.
VASE LIFE: 3 to 5 days, sometimes less.
AVAILABILITY: Daffodils and narcissus are available from winter through spring. Paperwhites are available at Christmas time, usually as potted plants. Bulbs are available in the fall for planting outdoors and forcing indoors.
COST: Winter—moderately priced. Spring—inexpensive.
ARRANGING TIP: Daffodils are best used alone unless properly conditioned. See care and conditioning tip 28.
GROWING TIP: Plant daffodils among other plants and bulbs in the garden. The bulbs and flowers are poisonous, and will help keep animals and pests from feasting on the garden. When picking daffodils, do not cut the foliage, but allow it to die back completely in order to nourish the bulbs for the next year's flowers. See growing tips 10, 11, and 12..

1a 1b 1c 2 3 4 5

1a, b, c. Dahlias may have single or multiple rows of petals. The blossoms range from small, ball types to large rays resembling daisies or peonies. Dahlias are available in dwarf sizes reaching only about a foot in height to taller varieties sometimes standing almost six feet, with blossoms about 16 inches across. Varieties pictured: a) pompon dahlia, b) decorative dahlia, c) cactus dahlia.

2. Buy fresh dahlias when they are three-fourths to fully open, with petals showing good color and no wilting outer petals.

3. Dahlias start to wilt from the outer petals toward the center. Check the backs of the flowers for freshness when purchasing. Dahlias wilt easily, so pulling off any foliage and buds helps the flower last longer. See care and conditioning tips 25 and 26.

4. Dahlias have attractive dark-green foliage and interesting offshoots of smaller blossoms and buds. However, they last longer if foliage and buds are removed. Save these when arranging. See arranging tips 6 and 16.

5. When dahlia flowers begin to wilt from the back, gently remove the outer wilted or discolored petals for a fresh-looking, smaller flower to use in arrangements.

NAMES: Dahlia.
VARIETIES: There are 28 species of dahlias and hundreds of varieties. These varieties are separated into 12 divisions, based on blossom type and shape.
COLORS: All shades and colors available, except no true blue. Many dahlias are striped or variegated. Some of the colors and combinations appear fluorescent, almost unreal.
SCENT: None.
FRESHNESS: Purchase or cut when the flowers are three-fourths to fully open. The outer petals should not be discolored or wilted.
VASE LIFE: Approximately 5 days, sometimes longer.
AVAILABILITY: Summer to early fall.
COST: Inexpensive.
ARRANGING TIP: Once dahlias start to wilt from the back, gently pull these petals off for a fresh-looking smaller flower.
GROWING TIP: Dahlias are prolific bloomers, producing many flowers throughout their season. Unlike most tuberous and bulb flowers, which give only a one-time show and rest until the next year, dahlias continue to bloom later than most flowers and offer a splash of color in the garden into fall. But they are very frost sensitive, so dig up the tubers just before the first frost and store until the next year for replanting. To grow large, showy flowers, see growing tip 18.
OTHER: See care and conditioning tips 25 and 26.

1. Delphiniums are tall flowers with spires of blossoms graduated up the stem. They have cup-shaped flowers that unfold into starlike blossoms. A fresh delphinium has three-fourths of its blossoms open, with only a few buds on the tip of the stem. The blossoms are just slightly up-facing, the stems erect, and the petals do not shed when handled.

2. Hybrid delphiniums (right) are the taller variety, with large blossoms very dense on thick, hollow stems. The belladonna variety (left) is similar but much shorter, with smaller blossoms spaced along the stem.

3. Older delphiniums have blossoms starting to turn downward. The flowers shed when handled.

4. Delphiniums add height to casual, airy bouquets, but can also be cut into two or three sections and used in fuller, more formal bouquets. This method allows one to use delphiniums in all types of arrangements.

NAMES: Delphinium.

VARIETIES: There are about 250 species of delphiniums. The most common are the large hybrid varieties known as English hybrids or *Delphinium elatum* and the smaller Belladonna varieties, or *Delphinium grandiflorum.* See photo 2.

COLORS: Predominantly shades of blue, violet, purple, and white. There is a rarer red-and-yellow variety. The hybrid varieties are available in blue and purple shades, but also in creams and pale pink. Delphiniums have dark or white small flower centers known as "bees."

SCENT: None.

FRESHNESS: Three-fourths of the blossoms are open, with just a few buds on the tip of the flower. Delphiniums in total bud will not fully open after being cut.

VASE LIFE: 5 to 7 days.

AVAILABILITY: All year, but the best season is early summer into fall.

COST: Hybrid varieties—moderately expensive to expensive. Others—inexpensive.

MEANING: The name *delphinium* is from the Greek word *delphis,* meaning dolphin, the buds being said to resemble a dolphin's snout.

NOTE: Some varieties are extremely poisonous.

ARRANGING TIP: Delphiniums are perfect for casual, airy garden bouquets, their tall spikes adding height. They can also be cut apart two to three times and used in more formal, full bouquets tucked in and around other flowers. See also arranging tips 13, 15, and 16.

GROWING TIP: The tall, majestic English hybrids or Pacific giant hybrids are called the "Queen of the border," sometimes reaching up to eight feet. These plants are perfect for the back of the garden. Delphiniums prefer the sunny locations, and are heavy feeders and drinkers. They thrive in cool, moist climates but also in areas with severe winters that reach as cold as 30 degrees below zero. Delphiniums bloom in early summer, but can be manipulated to bloom again in the fall. They are classified as perennials, but lose their vigor after about four or five years and must be replaced. Stake delphiniums as the bloom stalks develop, as they can easily break when the first wind comes along. See growing tip 16.

OTHER: See care and conditioning tips 8, 24, 29, 30, and 31.

1. Eremuri are very tall spiked flowers with multiflowered small starlike blossoms. The stems can reach three feet to sometimes nine feet in height. A fresh eremurus will have about one-third of its flowers open, with the majority of the blossoms in bud. The buds should show good color, and the tip of the flower should be tightly budded.

2. An older eremurus will have about three-fourths of its flowers open. The bottom blossoms will be discolored and dried.

3. Eremurus has a very long vase life as a cut flower. The bottom blossoms do die before the top of the flower blooms, and should be removed to encourage the others to open. This flower will appear almost half naked when the spent blossoms are gone. Wait a few days for the flower to fill out again, or cut down to suit its new proportions. Leaving the bottom blossoms attached may inhibit the others from blooming.

4. As eremurus ages and spent blossoms are removed, this striking flower can be cut down and used as a festive touch in mixed arrangements. As the flower develops further, and more blossoms open and fill out, it can be used alone again or combined with new flowers in another arrangement. With proper care, eremurus can last for weeks.

NAMES: Eremurus, Foxtail Lily, Desert Candle.
COLORS: Shades of yellow are most common, but eremuri are also available in oranges, pinks, and white.
SCENT: Very faint to none.
FRESHNESS: When the bottom third of the flowers has opened. The middle of the stem will have buds showing good color, and the tips will be tightly budded.
VASE LIFE: 10 to 14 days or longer.
AVAILABILITY: Early spring through summer.
COST: Moderately expensive.
ARRANGING TIP: Eremuri are very tall and long-lasting, an excellent choice for arranging. Use fresh eremuri for their height in flower arrangements. As the bottom blossoms fade and are pinched away, cut the stem down and reuse in medium or short combinations. With proper care, eremuri can last as long as three weeks, and can be enjoyed at all stages. See also arranging tip 15.
GROWING TIP: Eremuri are mostly grown by professionals for the cut flower trade and are rarely used as a garden plant. The spectacular tall spikes bloom in early spring, reaching up to as much as nine feet in height. This flower blooms before most of the other tall plants in the garden, so you can have a striking early border for other spring bulbs. Eremuri can last up to three weeks in the garden. The first shoots that appear in the early spring are frost sensitive, so cover with protective mulch until frost is no longer a danger. See growing tip 12.
OTHER: See care and conditioning tips 20, 24, and 29.

1. *Euphorbia fulgens* are large sprays of small flowers along a two- to three-foot curved stem. This variety is the most popular for flower arrangements. Flowers should be mostly open, with no signs of bruising. Flowers bruise easily when handled.

2. *Euphorbia marginata,* more commonly known as snow-on-the-mountain, is a variety predominantly used for its foliage. The small white flowers at the tip of the bright green leaves are said to resemble snow at the top of a mountain.

3. Some varieties of euphorbia, such as *Euphorbia characias,* resemble bright green cacti.

4. Euphorbias secrete a white milky sap when cut, which will cloud the water in arrangements. Change the water often and keep the vase flushed out regularly to prolong vase life. Use warmer water when conditioning or arranging. Cut the ends and place in very warm to hot water for a few minutes. The sap will secrete as water penetrates the stems, then place the stems in fresh, cooler water without recutting. The water will be clean and the end partly sealed.

NAMES: Euphorbia, Spurge.
VARIETIES: There are close to 8,000 species. The three most common varieties appreciated for their decorative flowers are *Euphorbia fulgens,* also called scarlet-plume (see photo 1); *Euphorbia marginata,* also known as snow-on-the-mountain (see photo 2); and *Euphorbia characias* (see photo 3).
COLORS: *Euphorbia fulgens* are available in orange, red, yellow, salmon, and white. Poinsettias are usually available in red, but also come in white, salmon, and pink shades. *Euphorbia marginata* is pale green with white variegations in the foliage and small white flowers at the top. *Euphorbia characias* is bright green with contrasting "eyes" or centers.
SCENT: None.
FRESHNESS: Most of the flowers are open. The leaves often wilt after these flowers are cut.
VASE LIFE: About a week.
AVAILABILITY: *Euphorbia marginata* is available all year. The other varieties are available late fall into early spring.
COST: *Euphorbia fulgens*—moderately expensive. *Euphorbia marginata*—inexpensive. *Euphorbia characias*—moderately expensive.
NOTE: Euphorbias secrete a poisonous milky sap that may cause skin irritation. Wear gloves when handling them. Euphorbias may also cause illness if ingested. The common pointsettia, a popular plant at Christmas time is also a type of euphorbia
ARRANGING TIP: When arranging with flowering euphorbia, it is wise to remove all the leaves from the stem, as they will quickly wilt. Try using cut poinsettia flowers at Christmas.
OTHER: See care and conditioning tip 27.

1. Flowering branches should be cut or purchased in bud stage. The buds should show good size and color, but even branches with tight buds will fully develop in time after being cut.

2. Older branches with fully opened flowers will shed when handled.

3. Using a few flowering branches in a flower arrangement adds height and texture, and acts as a natural brace for other flowers to rest against. Arrange with branches when they are in bud stage, before they begin to shed.

4. Fruit and berried branches can also be used as cut flowers. The fruit adds interesting texture to the flower combinations, as these crab apples do when combined with peach-colored lilies.

NAME: Flowering Branches.

VARIETIES: Any fruit tree or flowering shrub branches. Some popular varieties for cut flowers include apple blossoms, forsythia, pear blossoms, cherry blossoms, quince blossoms.

COLORS: Most flowering fruit branches have blossoms of white or shades of pink. Forsythia has small, starlike yellow blossoms.

SCENT: Most fruit tree blossoms have a wonderful fresh, sweet scent.

FRESHNESS: Purchase or cut when the blossoms are in bud stage. The flowers will slowly open and develop.

VASE LIFE: 10 days or more.

AVAILABILITY: Predominantly spring, but some flowering branches are available for sale in the winter. Also see growing tip below.

COST: Spring—moderately priced. Winter—moderately expensive.

MEANING: Apple blossoms are symbolic of preference; orange blossoms symbolize fertility and are commonly used in wedding ceremonies; peach blossoms mean "I am your captive." Quince blossoms symbolize temptation.

ARRANGING TIP: Flowering branches are very useful in large arrangements, adding texture and supplying a base for other flowers to brace against. Fruited or berried branches can also add interesting color and texture to a bouquet. See arranging tips 9 and 16.

GROWING TIP: Flowering branches are abundant in the spring, but it is easy to force them to bloom before their time by bringing dormant branches indoors. Clip branches in February and March to ensure they have endured a sufficient cold period for flowering. Place them in tepid water and place in low light. Once the buds develop, bring to a brighter spot for the blossoms to open. Change the water during this time of development. Be patient. Forcing branches can take some time, but the buds will eventually develop.

OTHER: See care and conditioning tips 5, 6, 20, and 24.

1. Forget-me-nots commonly grow in damp meadows and streambeds. Create such an environment for them after they are cut or purchased by submersing them in deep, cool water. This will harden the flowers and stems to enable them to be used in arrangements. If the stems become limp a few days later, use this method to recondition them.

2. Forget-me-nots are small, sky-blue flowers with yellow centers that bloom in small clusters along succulent green stems. Fresh forget-me-nots should have only a few flowers open, with several buds to blossom.

3. Older forget-me-nots have most of their flowers open. Some of the flowers may be dried out. Flowers drop from the stems when handled.

4. For the ultimate romantic bouquet, pair deep red roses with bright-blue forget-me-nots.

NAMES: Forget-me-not, Myosotis, Scorpion Grass.
COLORS: Bright-blue flowers with tiny yellow centers. White and pink varieties are sometimes available.
SCENT: None.
FRESHNESS: Cut or purchase when only a few flowers are open. Flowers should not shed when handled.
VASE LIFE: If fresh and conditioned properly, flowers will last 5 to 7 days or more.
AVAILABILITY: From March to May.
COST: Inexpensive.
MEANING: Remember me forever! Forget-me-nots are symbolic of true love.
ARRANGING TIP: These flowers do best in deep water, so use them tucked into the base of arrangements close to the water level. See arranging tip 12.
GROWING TIP: Once established, forget-me-nots need very little care and will multiply and spread quickly. They like gentle shade and moist conditions, so plant them in and around trees to naturalize for a striking blue carpet. Forget-me-nots also make a nice ground cover for spring bulbs. The bright-blue color accents other spring flowers and camouflages the spent foliage once the bulbs have bloomed.

1. Foxgloves are tall flowers with several drooping bell-shaped blossoms growing densely on a stem. The blossoms have dark spots in the throat, which guide bees to the center of the flower for pollination. A fresh foxglove has one-third of its bottom blossoms open, with the rest in bud. The tip is tightly budded, developing and blossoming after it has been cut with proper care. The flower stalk is firm and upright.

2. An older foxglove has faded blossoms on the bottom of its stem, and the tip of the flower may begin to droop. These blossoms can be removed and the stems recut to recondition the flower.

3. With their graceful appearance, foxgloves add the perfect long-lasting, old-fashioned touch to arrangements.

NAMES: Foxglove, Digitalis.
VARIETIES: The most common variety is known as *Digitalis purpurea.*
COLORS: Mostly white and shades of pink, lavender, and yellow. The throat of the flower is accented with dark spots.
SCENT: None.
FRESHNESS: The bottom third of the bell-shaped blossoms are open.
VASE LIFE: 10 days or longer.
AVAILABILITY: Late spring through summer.
COST: Moderately priced.
MEANING: The name *digitalis* comes from the Latin word for "finger." The flower got its informal name from the legend that fairies gave these blossoms to the foxes to wear on their claws for gloves, so they would not get caught when raiding the chicken coop. Foxgloves are symbolic of insincerity.
NOTE: The entire plant is poisonous. However, the dried leaves are used in the production of digitalis, an important cardiovascular medicine.
GROWING TIP: Most varieties of foxglove only have blossoms on one side of the stem. Because of this and height considerations, foxgloves are best grown against a wall or some type of background. If this flower is happy where it is planted, it will return year after year, but its temperamental nature makes it a little unpredictable. Foxgloves prefer partial shade. These plants bloom in late spring to early summer and can be fooled to bloom again in the fall. See growing tip 16.
OTHER: Foxgloves have very thick, dense stems, so they need to be recut often to prevent stem blockage. See also care and conditioning tips 24 and 29.

1

2

3

4

1. Freesias are dainty flowers with small, arching, fragrant blossoms atop very thin stems. They have long, bladelike leaves that are usually stripped away before sale. Freesias usually have 8 to 12 buds to a stem and are about 12 inches in length.

2. Cut or purchase freesias in bud stage with only the bottom blossom beginning to open and the next two or three blossoms of good size and showing color. These blossoms will open consecutively, but the tightly budded tips will not open fully and produce flowers.

3. Older freesias have the bottom two or three blossoms open; these may appear wrinkled and soft to the touch.

4. Freesia blossoms wilt from the bottom blossom up. When these spent blossoms are pinched off, the flower looks almost half-naked. Try attaching two older freesias in opposite directions to achieve a full-looking flower for arranging.

NAMES: Freesia.
VARIETIES: Freesia hybrids in single and double varieties.
COLORS: Available in most colors, except no true blue.
SCENT: Very sweet, almost fruity fragrance.
FRESHNESS: The end bud is just opening or ready to open, with the other three or four good-size buds showing color. The tip is green and tightly budded.
VASE LIFE: 5 to 7 days.
AVAILABILITY: All year.
COST: Moderately priced.
MEANING: Innocence.
ARRANGING TIP: Freesia blossoms wilt from the bottom blossom up. When these spent blossoms are pinched off, the flower looks almost half-naked. Try attaching two freesia in opposite directions to achieve a fuller-looking flower for arranging.
GROWING TIP: Freesia bulbs can be forced indoors in containers, but these little flowers require much more time and care to flower than other types of bulbs. Freesias need a strong light source during the day and cool nighttime temperatures. If exposed to the right conditions, they will produce flowers in four or five months from planting. The wait is worth the delightful scent. See growing tips 10 and 11.
OTHER: See care and conditioning tip 24.

1. *Fritillaria imperialis* is a large flower with a circle of hanging bell-type blossoms topped with a distinctive crown of foliage. The stem usually reaches two to three feet in height. Most of the flowers should be open. Unfortunately, this striking variety gives off an unpleasant odor.

2. The Meleagris variety has small, nodding bell-shaped blossoms with a quaint check pattern. These are about a foot high. The blossoms should be open or just beginning to crack.

3. *Fritillaria persica* has striking tall spires of deep purple, almost black bells blooming densely along the stem. This variety reaches two to four feet. About three-fourths of the flowers will be open, with just a few on the tip to bloom.

4. *Fritillaria milkowski* are small brown bells with gold tips. This variety reaches 8 to 12 inches in height. The blossoms should be open.

5. *Fritillaria* are among the most unusual flowers to use as an accent in the garden and in arrangements. Their unique shapes and colors add an unexpected touch. The small bells of *Fritillaria milkowski* are the perfect accent to these dark tulips with their similar shapes and colors.

NAME: Fritilaria.
VARIETIES: *Fritillaria imperialis,* also called crown-imperial lily or pineapple lily. See photo 1. *Fritillaria Meleagris* is also known as the snake's-head flower, guinea-hen tulip, or checkerboard lily. See photo 2. *Fritillaria persica,* see photo 3. *Fritillaria milkowski,* see photo 4.
COLORS: The imperialis variety is usually available in oranges, reds, and yellow. The Meleagris variety comes in unusual shades of cream to a pale maroon with a darker check pattern and is also available in pure white. The persica variety has deep purple to almost black flowers. The milkowski variety is brown with gold tips.
SCENT: Some varieties have an almost unpleasant musk odor.
FRESHNESS: Most of the flowers will be open. They show good color, becoming transparent with age.
VASE LIFE: Imperialis variety, 7 days or longer; the Meleagris and milkowski varieties, 3 to 5 days; the persica variety, 5 to 7 days. Remember to change the water frequently to prevent the flowers from developing an unpleasant odor.
AVAILABILITY: March to May.
COST: Imperialis and persica varieties—expensive. Meleagris and milkowski varieties—moderately priced.
GROWING TIP: All the varieties, with their distinctive shapes and colors, make fine accent flowers for the garden, especially the deep-colored persica when planted with daffodils and tulips. The bulbs are poisonous, so they also aid in keeping pests away from the garden. The unpleasant odor of *Fritillaria imperialis* is said to deter pests as well. See growing tip 12.
OTHER: See care and conditioning tip 28.

1. The most common geraniums are zonal geraniums. They are popular to grow in containers and window boxes outdoors in the summer. Zonal geraniums are characterized by large clusters of small flowers atop branching stems. The leaves are round, with darker-green horseshoe markings.

2. Martha Washington geraniums are another variety mostly grown as a container plant. The flowers are larger and are bicolored or have decorative stripes in the petals. Martha Washingtons need cooler temperatures to flower, unlike the other varieties, so grow this type as an indoor house plant in a sunny window if evening temperatures stay below 60 degrees.

3. Scented geraniums are grown for their fragrant leaves. These plants do not produce very showy flowers, but they come in many types of fragrance, which develop when the leaves are rubbed or cut. Scented geraniums are popular for making potpourri and flavorings for cooking.

4. Predominantly grown as an outside plant, geraniums are wonderful cut and mixed into summer bouquets for their intense color, pleasant fragrance, and lasting ability as a cut flower. Scented geraniums offer fragrant foliage for flower arrangements, especially when they are paired with flowers lacking their own scent. Here, scented geranium is paired with colorful ranunculus.

NAMES: Geranium, Pelargonium.
VARIETIES: Zonal geranium, photo 1; Martha Washington geranium, photo 2; scented geraniums, photo 3.
COLORS: White, shades of pink, peach, and red. Some of the colors seem almost fluorescent because of their bright, rich tones. The Martha Washington variety has bicolors or variegations through the petals.
SCENT: Very fragrant musk smell. The scented geraniums come in fragrances of lemon, rose, nutmeg, and even chocolate.
FRESHNESS: A few flowers are opening on the cluster, with more buds showing good color.
VASE LIFE: 10 days to 2 weeks or longer.
AVAILABILITY: Summer.
COST: Inexpensive.
ARRANGING TIP: Geraniums can be cut for summer bouquets to add intense color and fragrance. They are long-lasting cut flowers. Use the scented leaves as a foliage substitute with flowers that have no fragrance. See arranging tip 16.
GROWING TIP: Geraniums are popular container plants, for they are easy to grow and produce flowers all season long. Geraniums are also easy to "winter over" until the next year. Bring your containers indoors for the winter and keep them in a place of low light that stays about 40 to 50 degrees. Prune back at least half of the plant. Water infrequently. In the spring, move the plant to warmer temperatures and more light, and water regularly. The plants will be ready for another season.
OTHER: See care and conditioning tip 24.

1. Gerberas are daisylike flowers atop tubular stems. Gerberas come in an enormous number of colors and combinations. They are commonly available in regular and mini sizes, but there are oversize ones as well.

2. A fresh gerbera is fully open and has firm petals facing somewhat upright, and a sturdy stem. The flowers show good color and no pollination.

3. The unique spider gerbera.

4. Older gerberas have petals facing slightly downward, and the middle shows pollination. The petals and stem are softer to the touch than fresh ones.

5. Gerberas added to any combination afford great color and fun, and give the bouquet an informal touch.

NAMES: Gerbera, Gerbera Daisy, Transvaal Daisy.

VARIETIES: Large flower varieties and the mini variety called Gemini. Both varieties come in single and double forms. An oversize variety has recently become available.

COLORS: There are hundreds of shades and color combinations, but no true blue or black. Many are two-toned or variegated, and they may have yellow or black centers.

SCENT: None.

FRESHNESS: The petals should be fully open, but facing slightly upward. The flower and stem should be firm to the touch. The center should show no pollination.

VASE LIFE: 5 to 7 days. The fuzzy stems decompose quickly in deep water, so place gerberas in only four to five inches of water when conditioning or arranging alone.

AVAILABILITY: All year.

COST: Moderate.

ARRANGING TIP: This bright, informal flower can be added to any combination for fun and color, but gerberas can also make a stunning color impact massed together. See pages 42 and 43, and arranging tips 13 and 18.

GROWING TIP: Gerberas can be purchased as potted plants, and will last about three weeks. In very warm climates, gerberas can be grown in the garden and will produce flowers all summer.

OTHER: To make sure gerbera stems remain straight, support the flower heads when conditioning in water. This can be done by placing a piece of chicken wire over a deep bucket, so that the heads are supported and the stems hang free into the water. Let the flowers hydrate this way for several hours. See also care and conditioning tips 31 and 33.

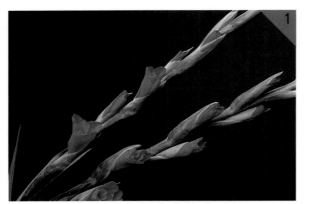

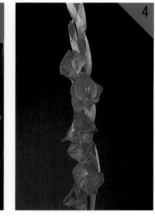

1. Gladioli are tall, dramatic flowers about two to three feet in height, covered with funnel-shaped blossoms just on one side of the stem that open from the bottom to the top. The leaves are long and swordlike in appearance. Fresh gladioli have a couple of open flowers at the base. These blossoms show no signs of drying around the edges. The next five or six buds are of a good size and color. The tip is tightly budded and will usually not open, and the bottom flowers die as the other ones develop.

2. A miniature variety, *Gladiolus orchideola,* to the left of the larger gladiolus, has smaller and fewer flowers along a narrow stem. The blossoms are spaced farther apart along the stem. Minature varieties are more supple and graceful in appearance, and are a better choice to use in mixed arrangements.

3. An unusual type of miniature gladiolus is known as *Gladiolus tristis.* It is a pale apple-green and emits a sweet scent only in the evening. Tristis blooms for just a short time in the summer.

4. Older gladioli have the bottom blossoms open, showing signs of age with dry edges, fading color and softness to the touch. When purchasing gladioli, check the bloom count to make sure these lower blooms have not been pinched away.

5. Several gladioli arranged together can take on an old-fashioned or a stark modern look. Gladioli arranged together best show the character of this flower.

NAMES: Gladiolus, Sword Lily.
VARIETIES: Larger flowering hybrid varieties (see photo 1) and smaller or miniature varieties. The most common of these are *Gladiolus colvillei* and *orchideola* (see photo 2). The miniature variety *Gladiolus tristis* is more uncommon (see photo 3).
COLORS: Almost every color shade is available, except for true blue. Bicolored and variegated varieties are also available.
SCENT: None, except for the miniature tristis variety.
FRESHNESS: The bottom one or two flowers are open, with five or six buds showing good color. The tip is tightly budded and does not usually develop after cutting. The bottom flowers die as the others open.
VASE LIFE: 10 days or longer.
AVAILABILITY: Available all year, but the predominant season is summer. The miniature varieties are only available in summer and early fall.
COST: Inexpensive.
ARRANGING TIP: These regal flowers can add height and drama to bouquets, but the stiffness of the flower makes it somewhat difficult to blend into a combination, and the bottom open blossoms are usually shadowed by other flowers. Gladioli are best appreciated when several are massed together. See also arranging tip 15.
OTHER: See care and conditioning tips 24 and 29.

1. Gloriosa are vibrant flowers with very reflexed petals growing along a climbing vine. The flowers are bright red and are striped with yellow on the outer petals. The flowers resemble lilies and are commonly referred to as gloriosa lilies. Fresh gloriosa are fully open, with no signs of pollination. The petals show good color and are firm to the touch.

2. Older gloriosa show age with drying or discoloration on the outer petals. The flowers are soft to the touch, and the overall color is fading.

3. This flower grows on a climbing vine and usually shows some of its spiral tendrils. Use these tendrils to attach to other flowers when arranging to give a climbing, draping effect.

4. Exotic gloriosa can be combined with old-fashioned garden flowers for added punch.

NAMES: Gloriosa, Gloriosa Lily, Vine Lily, Rothschild Lily.
VARIETIES: *Gloriosa Rothschildiana.*
COLORS: Bright red with vibrant yellow stripes on the outer edges of the petals; an orange variety is sometimes available.
SCENT: None.
FRESHNESS: The flowers are fully open. They are usually sold as short stems with single blossoms cut from the vine, and as long vine stems with usually two to three flowers and a few pale or green small flowers. These smaller flowers do not fully develop after they are cut.
VASE LIFE: 5 to 7 days or longer.
AVAILABILITY: All year.
COST: Short stems—moderately priced. Long vine stems—expensive.
ARRANGING TIP: Unlike most branching vines, these flowers have some lasting power after they are cut and the blooms are not separated from the stem. Use this vibrant vine draped around the base of just about any combination. The tropical appearance of this flower allows it to mix even with old-fashioned types of flowers. The vines usually have some of the tiny tendrils that the flower uses for climbing, and these can be used to attach the vine to other flowers to give a climbing effect in an arrangement. See arranging tip 1.
OTHER: This flower only grows in very warm, humid situations. Frequent misting with tepid water helps prolong its vase life.

1. Heather is a low-growing shrub with branches consisting of dozens of tiny bell-shaped flowers. Fresh heather has most of the blossoms open and showing good color, and the flowers do not shed when handled.

2. Aged heather sheds when handled. The color is somewhat faded and the blossoms may feel dry to the touch. This flower dries naturally with age. Spraying the flower with hair spray may keep it from shedding.

3. Heather is best arranged in a grouping of stems to show off the vibrant color and texture. Used sparingly, it can give a weedy look to arrangements. Here, deep magenta heather is stuffed around bright red roses, the two colors and textures nicely accenting one another.

NAMES: Heather, Heath.
VARIETIES: Calluna, Erica, Daboecia.
COLORS: Mostly pink, but some varieties are available in cream and white.
SCENT: None.
FRESHNESS: When most of the blossoms are open, the tip of the flower is still budded. The flowers do not shed when handled.
VASE LIFE: Approximately 5 days. Heather will eventually dry and can be used out of water.
AVAILABILITY: All year, but predominantly in winter and spring.
COST: Inexpensive.
ARRANGING TIP: Heather is mostly associated with the hillsides of England, displaying an intense carpet over the landscape. When arranging with heather, keep this concept in mind, because while the mass of color is intense, when separated it almost gets lost. This flower is best arranged in large groupings to display its true color and texture. See also arranging tip 12.
OTHER: Frequent misting helps prolong freshness. As heather ages, try some hair spray to help prevent shedding. See care and conditioning tip 4.

1. Grape hyacinths, also known as muscari, are a related variety that is much smaller. They have a mild, sweet fragrance.

2. Dutch hyacinths are cone-shaped with numerous florets dense on the stem. A fresh hyacinth has most of its florets closed, with only a few opening at the base. The color is strong, the scent sweet.

3. Older hyacinths have most of their florets open. The color is faded and the scent is very strong.

4. Hyacinths have a thick, fibrous base. This is the white part of the stem and should be cut off before putting hyacinths in water. The water will then be able to penetrate the stem and reach the flowers.

5. One hyacinth bulb forced in a glass: a perfect way to really appreciate this flower.

NAMES: Hyacinth or Dutch Hyacinth; Grape Hyacinth or Muscari.
VARIETIES: *Hyacinth orientalis,* available in single and double varieties. The most common grape hyacinth is the *Muscari armeniacum.*
COLORS: Available in a variety of colors—pinks, cream, white, purples—but the most common are the blue shades.
SCENT: Very sweet fragrance that becomes stronger with age as more of the florets open.
FRESHNESS: Purchase or cut flowers when the florets are mostly closed.
VASE LIFE: 7 to 10 days or longer.
AVAILABILITY: October to May.
COST: Winter—moderately expensive. Spring—moderately priced.
MEANING: Remembrance. It was common to engrave these flowers onto gravestones.
NOTE: Hyacinths are poisonous. Remember to wear gloves when working with them, because of their poisonous latex. When planting hyacinths, handling the bulbs may cause an itchy reaction.
ARRANGING TIP: This beautiful flower changes so much in its cycle that one can appreciate it best when it stands alone.
GROWING TIP: Hyacinths are wonderful to grow inside in the wintertime. See also growing tips 10, 11, and 12.
OTHER: See also care and conditioning tip 28.

1a

1b

1c

2

3

4

1a, b, c. Hydrangeas are a shrub with flowers consisting of large, lush clusters of many blossoms. The three most common types are a) the large, full-headed variety, known as a mop head (the most popular); b) the disk-shaped variety with loose, graceful clusters of flowers consisting mostly of small closed buds, known as the lace cap; and c) the cream-colored, cone-shaped hydrangea with full, elongated blossoms, known as the panicle hydrangea.

2. A fresh hydrangea has most of the flowers in the cluster open, except for the lace cap variety. The flower is sturdy and firm to the touch.

3. Aged hydrangeas have some of the blossoms on the cluster wilted, and the overall flower feels soft to the touch.

4. Hydrangeas benefit from extra conditioning. Drape cold, wet cloths over the top of the blossoms after they are cut.

NAMES: Hydrangea.
VARIETIES: *Hydrangea macrophylla,* which includes the mop heads and lace cap varieties, and *Hydrangea paniculata,* from which the cone-shaped variety is developed. The latter is sometimes referred to as a PeeGee or P.G. hydrangea (from paniculata grandiflora).
COLORS: Pale to intense shades of blue, purple, pink, white, green, and some deep burgundy shades. Some varieties produce two-tone colors.
SCENT: None.
FRESHNESS: Most of the flowers are open and firm to the touch.
VASE LIFE: If conditioned properly, 5 to 7 days or longer.
AVAILABILITY: Summer into early fall.
COST: Moderately expensive.
MEANING: Perseverance.
ARRANGING TIP: These large blossoms are wonderful for creating a colorful base for arrangements. The flower acts as a big cushion, holding other flowers in place as you build your arrangement. See arranging tip 14. Hydrangeas cut in the late summer and fall may dry naturally, holding their color and shape.
OTHER: Hydrangeas wilt easily when cut. They benefit from special care and conditioning for prolonged vase life. Place the ends of the stems in boiling water, being careful to protect the blossoms from the steam. Place the boiled end, approximately 1 inch, into powdered alum (available at most grocery stores). Gently tap the excess powder from the stem ends and place in deep, cool water. Drape the top of the blossoms with a cold wet cloth, keeping the cloth moist by misting frequently during the conditioning period—about four hours. This helps harden the blossoms. See also care and conditioning tips 4, 25, 26, and 32.

1. Hypericum berries are large clusters of deep-brown branching berries atop slender, woody stems. The berries should be large and full, with a smooth, firm appearance. The berries also come in shades of pink and peach and deep burgundy.

2a, b. Older hypericum berries are wrinkled and soft to the touch. They may also change color with age.

3. Hypericum berries are wonderful accents for fall and winter bouquets. Most berries drop from the branches when handled or with age, but hypericum berries stay attached to the stem, making them easy to use in arrangements.

NAMES: Hypericum, Hypericum Berries, St.-John's-Wort.
VARIETIES: *Hypericum perforatum.*
COLORS: The flowers are tiny golden yellow, but this plant is mostly sold for its large, decorative clusters of berries in shades of brown, peach, pale pink, and deep burgundy.
SCENT: None.
FRESHNESS: The berries show good size and color, and feel firm to the touch.
VASE LIFE: The berries will last 7 to 10 days or longer.
AVAILABILITY: All year.
COST: Moderately priced.
NOTE: Hypericum or St.-John's-wort is widely used as a natural treatment for depression and to promote well-being.
ARRANGING TIP: Hypericum berries are wonderful to use in arrangements, because the berries stay on the stems.
OTHER: See care and conditioning tips 5 and 6.

1a, b, c. Iris are exotic flowers, with intensely colored blossoms of unusual shape. The flower is made up of three inner petals arching up and three outer petals falling down. The three most common varieties are the florist iris known as a) Dutch iris, the more graceful b) Siberian iris, and the large, showy variety known as the c) bearded iris. The bearded iris has a fuzzy, brightly colored strip along the fallen lower petals known as the beard. This little beard attracts bees to the flower for pollination.

2. *Iris reticulata* is a miniature variety that only reaches some four to six inches in height. This variety can also be forced to bloom inside in the winter months.

3. Iris should always be cut or purchased when in total bud stage. The flowers open quickly and last only a few days. The bud should be of good size and color and feel firm to the touch. If the tip is discolored or dry, the flower will not open.

4. Aged iris are fully open, and their tips may have started to dry and discolor.

5. Iris blossoms are beautiful arranged in their natural state, but also do well combined with other flowers as an accent of vibrant color and texture. Their unique shape and form allows proper spacing for other flowers to be added in and around them to form an arrangement.

NAMES: Iris, Fleur-de-Lis.
VARIETIES: The common Dutch iris, the large flowered bearded variety, and the Siberian iris.
COLORS: Most shades and combinations. The inner part of the flower and the outer petals are sometimes accented with different colors and combinations than the predominant color of the flower. The Dutch variety is most common in dark blue and purple accented with yellow.
SCENT: Only a few varieties have a sweet scent; the common iris has no scent.
FRESHNESS: Purchase or cut in bud stage. Iris open quickly and the flowers do not last long.
VASE LIFE: 3 to 5 days.
AVAILABILITY: The predominant season is late spring and early summer, but the Dutch variety is available as a cut flower all year.
COST: Inexpensive to moderately priced.
MEANING: "I have a message for you."
ARRANGING TIP: Iris flowers, with their unique shape and form, can be useful in arrangements by accenting other flowers. The shape allows other flowers to rest next to the iris blossoms. See arranging tip 13.
GROWING TIP: Iris multiply rapidly and reach their flowering peak about the third year after planting, so they must be divided every few years to continue flowering. The foliage will not discolor or fade after the flowers have bloomed. The tall, swordlike blades will stay green and are an attractive accent in the garden. See growing tips 10, 11, 12, and 19.

1. Lady's mantles are small, tiny rosettes of chartreuse green flowers atop large, lush round leaves. Fresh lady's mantle will have the rosettes tight; the color will be a strong chartreuse green.

2. Aged lady's mantles have the rosettes more spread apart and the chartreuse has faded to a more yellow color. The tips of the tiny flowers may have started to brown.

3. The light, airy texture of lady's mantle makes this an easy flower to add to arrangements, because it can be clumped together to fill tiny gaps as well as spread apart for use as a filler in bouquets. The bright color accents other flowers and is also a nice choice when arranging with one type of flower and just a little something extra is needed.

NAMES: Lady's Mantle, Alchemilla.
VARIETIES: *Alchemilla mollis.*
COLORS: Chartreuse.
SCENT: None.
FRESHNESS: The flowers have tight rosettes and strong color.
VASE LIFE: Approximately 7 days.
AVAILABILITY: The predominant season is summer, but sometimes lady's mantle is available in late spring as well.
COST: Moderately priced.
NOTE: The large leaves of alchemilla were said to resemble a lady's cloak, thus the informal name lady's mantle. The leaves collect dewdrops in the early morning, which were thought to have magical powers.
ARRANGING TIP: Lady's mantle, with its light and airy texture, can be used as a light filler in loose arrangements or clumped together to fill in small gaps in tight arrangements. The bright green color adds a subtle accent to any arrangement. See also arranging tips 8 and 12.
GROWING TIP: Lady's mantle is wonderful to grow in the garden for its bright green flowers, and it also makes a fine ground cover after the flowers have faded. The large green leaves make a thick, lush carpet in the garden all summer and are a nice way to hide unattractive foliage from faded plants such as bulbs, etc. Lady's mantle is very easy to grow, needing little attention and tolerating full shade to partial sun. It is a reliable perennial, becoming stronger every year. The leaves collect and hold dewdrops in the morning, giving the garden a glistening effect.

1. Liatris are tall, narrow spike flowers consisting of dozens of tiny fuzzy blossoms graduating down the stem. Liatris are unusual in that they blossom from the top of the flower downward. The leaves are thin and grasslike. Fresh liatris have the top one or two inches of the flower's blossoms open, with the middle of the flower showing good size and color. The bottom blossoms do not fully develop after liatris are cut.

2. Older liatris have about half of the flowers open, and the tips are discolored and dry. The bottom, undeveloped blossoms may also have a dried appearance.

3. Liatris add instant color to tall combinations, because the flowers open from tip to base. They are a versatile choice—useful in exotic bouquets as well as in more casual arrangements.

NAMES: Liatris, Gay Feather, Blazing Star.
COLORS: Shades of purple and magenta.
SCENT: None.
FRESHNESS: The top one or two inches of flower buds are open, the middle of the flower is budded and showing good color.
VASE LIFE: 7 days or longer.
AVAILABILITY: All year.
COST: Inexpensive.
ARRANGING TIP: Tall, slender, sturdy liatris add a touch of intense color to tall combinations. The flowers are nonobstructive in that they do not change rapidly or shift in their aging cycle. The flowers start opening from the top downward, unlike most tall flowers whose blossoms open from the base upward. Since the flowers open from the tip, liatris add instant color and texture. They go beautifully with exotic flowers such as lilies and orchids, and also blend into more casual combinations with delphinium and iris.
GROWING TIP: Liatris are very easy to grow and make a nice addition to the garden, because of their intense color and the ability to blend with exotic blooms as well as field flowers. The tall, colorful stems can tolerate sun or partial shade and do not need much space. Plant in clumps for the showy, intense color, or scatter in and around other flowers for splashes of color.
OTHER: Liatris pollute the water very quickly, so be sure to strip all the thin bladelike leaves that fall below the waterline and change the water frequently. See care and conditioning tip 8.

1. Lilacs are hardy shrubs with dense clusters of fragrant flowers. They should be cut or purchased when most of the blossoms are open. Lilacs cut in the tight budded stage will most likely not open. The clusters of flowers should be upright and firm to the touch.

2. Lilacs are a short-lived cut flower—the clusters will wilt within a few days. Check closely to make sure that the flowers are not drooping or soft to the touch.

3. This unusual two-tone variety is called sensation.

4. One way to prolong the vase life of lilacs is by changing or flushing the water frequently. Lilacs respond to warm, almost hot water. Try doing this if the flowers seem to be wilting. The fresh, heady scent of lilacs is worth the extra effort.

NAMES: Lilac, Syringa.
VARIETIES: *Syringa vulgaris,* single and double varieties.
COLORS: Shades of lavender, purple, rosy pink, and white.
SCENT: Strong, sweet fragrance.
FRESHNESS: Most of the flowers are open, or beginning to open. If flowers are cut too early, and are mostly budded, they probably will not open.
VASE LIFE: Approximately 3 to 5 days, sometimes less.
AVAILABILITY: Lilacs bloom only in the spring, but an imported French hybrid variety is available from florists starting in late December through the winter. This variety is not very fragrant.
COST: Winter—expensive. Spring—moderately priced.
MEANING: Lilacs symbolize first love.
ARRANGING TIP: Lilacs mixed into spring bouquets have exquisite scent and color, but unfortunately these flowers last longer when used alone. See arranging tips 8 and 14.
GROWING TIP: Properly pruning lilac shrubs will produce more flowers for the next year. Trim all lilac flowers after they have faded, just below the end of the flower sprig. Also, trim away some of the older branches that bend close to the ground. This will ensure plenty of blossoms for the next year. Do not prune your lilac after the Fourth of July. At this point, lilacs are beginning their new growth, and pruning may inhibit next season's show of blossoms.
OTHER: See care and conditioning tips 5, 6, and 32.

1a, b, c. Lilies are large, star-shaped flowers with two to as many as five or six branching blossoms to a stem. The three most common varieties are a) Asiatic, b) Oriental, and c) longiflorum lilies; the last-named are also known as the Easter lily.

2. It is important to remove the stamens from lily buds when they open. This helps the flower last longer, by tricking it into staying in bloom in hopes of getting fertilized. If left intact, the stamens will pollinate and may stain the flower and other things as well. Use a fork to lift stamens gently away from the lily if they are starting to pollinate.

3. A fresh lily has only the bottom blossom open, with the next two to three consecutive buds showing good size and color. Lilies bruise easily because of their large, branching shape, so check for damage and discoloration on the closed blossoms.

4. Older lilies have most of the blossoms fully open except for the budded top. The blossoms may appear faded or slightly transparent. Some of the bottom blossoms may have been pinched away, so check the stem and bloom count before purchasing.

5. A recently developed lily nicknamed the LA lily is a hybrid developed from a cross between the longiflorum lily and the Asiatic lily. It combines the vibrant colors and shades of the Asiatic lilies with larger, showier blossoms of the longiflorum variety.

NAMES: Lily, Lilium.
VARIETIES: There are seven divisions or types of lilies, made up of over 400 species. The three most common varieties are Asiatic lilies, Oriental lilies, and longiflorum lilies.
COLORS: The Asiatic varieties come in almost every color and shade except blue and black. The Oriental varieties mostly come in shades of white, cream, and pink. Both of these varieties may be solid, or accented with spots, stripes, or contrasting colors in the throat of the flower. The longiflorum lily is pure white.
SCENT: The Oriental varieties have a strong fragrance, the Easter lily or longiflorum lily a slight fragrance. The Asiatic varieties are scent-free.
FRESHNESS: Purchase or cut when the bottom flower is just opening and the next two or three buds are full and showing good color.
VASE LIFE: 10 days or longer.
AVAILABILITY: All year, but the predominant season is spring and summer.
COST: Oriental—expensive. Others—moderately priced.
MEANING: Purity and sweetness.
ARRANGING TIP: Do not crowd lilies in arrangements, as the large blossoms need room to open up. See arranging tips 8, 13, 14, 15, and 16.
GROWING TIP: Lilies prefer full sun, but also like cold feet. Plant where they will receive afternoon shade to cool their roots. See also growing tip 12.
OTHER: Lilies do not like flower preservative or additives in the water. See care and conditioning tips 24, 29, and 31.

1. Lilies of the valley are clusters of tiny white bell flowers hanging from a single stem. The flowers are surrounded by their large, pointed, deep-green leaves. Flowers should be cut or purchased when most of the blossoms are fully open, with just a few buds on top. The fragrance is pleasantly strong.

2. Older lilies of the valley have flowers beginning to dry out and brown around the edges. The fragrance is mild to none.

3. The stems of lilies of the valley are connected and enclosed by the base of their leaves. Gently pull this connection apart and recut the stems and leaf base before putting in water. The flowers will last longer.

4. The scent of lilies of the valley is so powerful that just a few flowers will fill a room with fragrance. Try some next to a bedside table or near a workplace. This little spring flower's perfume is a great escape.

NAMES: Lily of the Valley, Convallaria.
VARIETIES: The single variety is most common and popular, but there is a double white variety as well.
COLORS: White, but sometimes pale pink varieties are available.
SCENT: Very fragrant. A few flowers can scent a room. Lily of the valley is widely used in the manufacture of perfume.
FRESHNESS: Most of the bell-shaped flowers are open, with just a few buds on top to bloom. If the flowers are closed on the stem when cut, they probably will not open.
VASE LIFE: 4 to 5 days.
AVAILABILITY: Lilies of the valley only bloom briefly in the spring, but they are available year round in limited quantities.
COST: Spring—moderately priced. Other seasons—very expensive.
MEANING: Happiness or the return of happiness.
ARRANGING TIP: Try just a few sprigs on your bedside table for sweet dreams. See also arranging tip 8.
GROWING TIP: Lilies of the valley prefer a shady spot in the garden. The plants will take a few years to establish and flower, so be patient. Lilies of the valley are worth the wait. Once established, they will thrive spring after spring. See growing tips 10, 11, and 12.
OTHER: See care and conditioning tip 34.

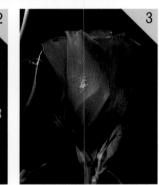

1. Lisianthus are cup-shaped flowers that bloom along thin, gracefully branching stems. They resemble a cross between a rose and a poppy. The stems usually bear three to five flowers along with several immature buds. The foliage is gray-green in color, with a waxy texture. A fresh lisianthus has two to three mature open flowers with a couple of fully developed buds to open. The open flowers show good color and no discoloration or bruising on the edges. The tips of the branching stems have a slight curve, but for the most part are upright.

2. Older lisianthus may show signs of age by the discoloration of the flower petal edges. The tips of the stems have a more extreme curve and feel soft to the touch.

3. Be careful not to let moisture remain on the flowers of lisianthus, because water spots will discolor the petals. Lisianthus are also prone to mildew.

4. Lisianthus are difficult to combine with other flowers. The structure of the flower is dense, with many branching blossoms, and when combined with other flowers the blossoms may appear crowded. Start the bouquet with a few lisianthus stems as a base. When adding other flowers, clip the branch of the lisianthus flower that is in the way, so to speak, and tuck other flowers into the new opening. Save the clipped blossoms and tuck them around the edges of the arrangement.

NAMES: Lisianthus.
VARIETIES: *Eustoma grandiflorum* varieties, single and double varieties.
COLORS: White, cream, pink, peach, lavender, purple, pale green, and some bicolors.
SCENT: None.
FRESHNESS: When a couple of the outer blossoms are fully open with a few more blossoms just opening. Watch for bruising and discoloration around the edges.
VASE LIFE: 7 to 10 days, sometimes longer.
AVAILABILITY: All year.
COST: Moderately priced.
ARRANGING TIP: Lisianthus can be difficult to arrange with other flowers, owing to their dense, branching stems. Fill a vase with a base of lisianthus, and gently clip away some of the branching stems for other flowers to be added. Lisianthus stems can also be separated and the flowers and blossoms used in shorter combinations. See arranging tips 8, 13, 16, and 18.
OTHER: As well as bruising easily, lisianthus are also prone to water spots, which look as though drops of bleach have spilled on the petals. See care and conditioning tips 24, 25, and 26.

1. Nerines consist of a cluster of about five or six small, lily-shaped flowers with reflexed petals atop a stark, dark-green leafless stem. A fresh nerine is mostly in bud, with the blossoms full and just opening at the tip of the bloom.

2. Older nerines have most of the blossoms open, and the tips of the flower may appear transparent or discolored.

3. Nerines have the great look, texture, and shape, of lilies without the size. They give combinations that exotic touch without the bulk.

NAMES: Nerine, Nerine Lily, Guernsey Lily.
VARIETIES: *Nerine Bowdenii* is the most common and available. Also available are *Nerine sarniensis* and *Nerine undulata*.
COLORS: Predominantly bright pink, but some varieties are white, cream, peach, orange, or crimson red.
SCENT: A very slight, unusual scent.
FRESHNESS: The blossoms are just starting to crack open, but the flowers are mostly still in bud.
VASE LIFE: 7 days or longer.
AVAILABILITY: Fall through winter.
COST: Moderately priced.
NOTE: Nerines were believed to have washed ashore on the English Channel island of Guernsey, where the flower was first discovered, thus the nickname Guernsey lily.
ARRANGING TIP: With their glistening color and texture, nerines look almost frosted. They are wonderful mixed with Christmas greens, since they are readily available in winter. See arranging tip 13.
GROWING TIP: Nerines are best grown as a container plant. They do not mind being crowded together, and will not need dividing for several years. The plants are very cold sensitive, so bring them indoors for the winter.

1 (opposite). There are thousands of species of orchids in many different shapes and sizes.

2a, b, c, d. The most common types available are a) Cymbidiums, b) Dendrobiums, c) Oncidiums, and d) Phalaenopsis. Phalaenopsis orchids are the best variety to grow as house plants.

3

4a

4b

5

6

3. Choose cut orchids by bloom size and color. Look for large blossoms in scale with stem size. Most of the blossoms should be open, as most varieties will not fully develop when cut. Orchids bruise easily, so check the blossoms before purchasing.

4a. Aged orchids usually have a yellow or faded tip where there are unopened blossoms .

4b. Some of the bottom blossoms may also be discolored or appear wrinkled and transparent.

5. In nature, orchids grow by attaching their roots above the ground. When growing them as houseplants, make sure that the roots are exposed to receive humidity and ventilation.

6. Orchids are a very versatile flower to use in arrangements because they can be paired with formal types of flowers for elaborate bouquets but work just as well with casual companions. White dendrobium orchids are paired here with Queen Anne's lace.

NAME: Orchid.

VARIETIES: There are over 30,000 varieties of orchid. The most common available as cut flowers and plants are Cymbidium, Dendrobium, Oncidium, and Phalaenopsis orchids.

COLORS: Every shade and color except true blue. Orchids can be solid colors, but are usually multi-colored, with spots or stripes accenting the throat of the blossom.

SCENT: Some varieties are fragrant, such as the Cymbidium.

FRESHNESS: Most of the flowers are open, or beginning to open. If cut too early while mostly budded, they probably will not open.

VASE LIFE: Approximately 7 days, but some varieties will last two weeks.

AVAILABILITY: All year.

COST: Moderately expensive to expensive, depending on the variety. Cymbidium and Phalaenopsis orchids are the most expensive cut varieties.

MEANING: Beautiful lady, Belle.

ARRANGING TIP: Orchids are very versatile in flower arranging, lending an exotic touch to any combination. Their amazing color combinations and lasting ability make them a good choice for flower arrangements. Long-stemmed orchids with multiple blossoms can be cut into two or three parts for use in arrangements. See Delphinium, photo 4 on page 78.

GROWING TIP: Most varieties like direct sun and warm, humid conditions, but some prefer more indirect light and cooler temperatures. One such is the Phalaenopsis orchid, which is a good variety to grow indoors under normal conditions. Plant in bark, stones, or moss, and place in high indirect or filtered light; the edges of the leaves will burn or brown if the orchid is receiving too much light. Water your orchid once a week by drenching the roots and draining completely. Orchids prefer humid conditions. Misting frequently and resting the pot on a few pebbles will produce this type of environment. Occasionally place a few ice cubes on top of the bark to let moisture slowly soak in and cool the roots. See also growing tips 4 and 5.

OTHER: Frequent misting of cut orchids will lengthen their vase life. See also care and conditioning tips 24, 29, and 34.

1. Peonies are large, lush blossoms that can be single, semidouble—or, most popular—double blossoms like the one pictured at left. This variety is also known as the bomb type, because of its round shape and explosion of multiple petals. The blossoms sometimes reach five to six inches across.

2. A fresh peony should be cut or purchased in bud stage, when the bud is about the size of a tennis ball and is semisoft to the touch—much like checking a peach for ripeness. Buds too firm to the touch will probably not develop. Peonies make excellent cut flowers when cut at the proper bud stage.

3. Aged peonies have most of their petals open and turned downward. The flower is soft to the touch, with some of the outer petals discolored. The flower may shed or falls apart when handled.

4. Peonies' dark-red shoots emerging in the spring do not at all resemble the large shrub that will develop in a few months. Peonies die all the way back to the ground in winter, replacing all foliage in the spring.

5. Arranging with peonies is easy. Just a few peonies can fill a vase, and few flowers are needed to complete a bouquet.

NAMES: Peony, Paeonia.
VARIETIES: Herbaceous varieties in single, semidouble, and double-bloom types.
COLORS: Shades of white, cream, peach, pink into deep crimson shades. Some varieties may be multicolored, with specks of contrasting color at the base of the flower's center.
SCENT: From sweet, mild fragrance to very aromatic, depending on the variety.
FRESHNESS: Purchase or cut when the flower is still in bud stage. See photo 2.
VASE LIFE: 7 to 10 days, or longer.
AVAILABILITY: Spring only, but some cut flowers are available from New Zealand in winter.
COSTS: Spring—moderately expensive. Winter—expensive.
MEANING: Bashfulness.
ARRANGING TIP: With blossoms reaching to sometimes 5 inches across, peonies are an arrangement in themselves. See arranging tips 8, 13, and 14.
GROWING TIP: For the best show of blooms, purchase tubers or plants with three to five eyes or growth shoots, since one- or two-eyed tubers or plants may take years to produce blossoms. See photo 4. Remember not to plant peonies too deep, or the plant will produce a show of leaves but no flowers. The eyes should only be about two inches below the soil level. Although they will tolerate partial shade, plant peonies in full sun, away from trees and other shrubs, so that the plants need not compete for nutrients. Bloom time for peonies is only a few weeks, so select early-, mid-, and late-blooming varieties. Be careful when cutting for arrangements—cutting more than one-third of the flowers produced will inhibit blossom count and size for the following year. Be patient; peonies usually take three to five years to reach maturity, but once established, will bloom forever.
OTHER: See care and conditioning tips 31, 32, and 34.

1. Phlox are large clusters of sweetly scented, disk-shaped flowers atop branching stems. A fresh phlox should be cut or purchased when two-thirds of the florets are open and the closed buds show good size and color. Those cut too early, in tight bud stage, will not develop.

2. Aged phlox have all of their blossoms open and many may have dropped. Older phlox shed when handled.

3. Phlox, with their large clusters of fragrant flowers, are a nice addition to combinations of large showy flowers, such as roses and peonies.

NAMES: Phlox.
VARIETIES: Garden phlox, phlox paniculata.
COLORS: Shades of white, pink, purple, red, and orange. The centers or eyes may have a contrasting color.
SCENT: Sweet, mild scent.
FRESHNESS: Purchase or cut when two-thirds of the blossoms are open on the cluster, with the remaining buds showing good size and color.
VASE LIFE: Approximately 10 days or longer.
AVAILABILITY: Summer.
COST: Moderately priced.
MEANING: Agreement.
ARRANGING TIP: With their large cluster of blossoms, phlox can be the main showy ingredient in a combination, or an accent for other large, showy flowers. See arranging tips 12, 13, and 14.
GROWING TIP: Phlox are very easy to grow, but be sure to remove the spent flower heads, as the dispersal of seed will create undesirable plants and may crowd out the main plant. Phlox also attract butterflies to the garden.
OTHER: See care and conditioning tip 24.

1a, b. Poppies are cup-shaped flowers with silky tissuelike petals that have a crinkled appearance. They grow from thin, spindly stems atop a clump of fernlike foliage. a) the Oriental variety is larger and taller, and usually has deep blue-black blotches at the base of the center.
b) Icelandic poppies are smaller and have golden centers.

2. Purchase or cut poppies in bud stage, but only if you can see some color peeking through. The outer shell will drop and the flower will pop open. Large, plump buds can be gently peeled apart to encourage the flower to open sooner. Poppy buds cut too tight will not open.

3. Aged poppies are fully open, with pollen forming in the center. The outer petals may have started to brown or discolor. The tissuelike petals may have become more transparent in appearance, and the flower may shed or fall apart when handled.

4. Poppy pods or the center of the poppy flower are attractive to use in dried or fresh arrangements after the petals have faded. Shake all the seeds out of the pods before using, to avoid a mess.

5. Poppies are great to use in combinations for their colors, fragrance, and texture. Closed poppy buds added to the top of this arrangement lend a whimsical touch.

NAMES: Poppy, Papaver.
VARIETIES: Oriental poppy, Icelandic poppy. Most are single-flowering varieties, but some are available in semidouble forms.
COLORS: The Icelandic variety is available in shades of white, yellow, pink, and orange. The Oriental variety is most popular in oranges and reds, but is also available in white and pink.
SCENT: Fresh, mild scent.
FRESHNESS: Purchase or cut in bud stage, but the bud must show some color of the blossom.
VASE LIFE: Approximately 3 to 5 days. Poppies must be seared on the ends and placed in warm water to be used as a cut flower. See care and conditioning tip 27.
AVAILABILITY: Early summer for the Oriental variety, all summer for the Icelandic type.
COST: Moderately priced.
MEANING: Consolation.
NOTE: Poppies are also associated with sleep, as the narcotic drug opium can be extracted from the latex of the young pods of a variety of Oriental poppy. Two important drugs manufactured from opium are widely used in treatment of pain—codeine and morphine. Poppies are also used in cooking, mainly in baked goods. The seeds are extracted and toasted before use. These seeds are not dangerous to consume.
ARRANGING TIP: Poppies at all stages can be used as accents in arrangements. See arranging tip 16.
OTHER: Poppies have fuzzy stems that quickly decompose in water, resulting in extra bacterial growth. Change the water frequently to prolong vase life. See also care and conditioning tip 31, and growing tip 20.

1a

1b

2

3

4

5

1a, b. Ranunculus are small, cup-shaped flowers similar in shape and texture to peonies and camellias. These flowers consist of several multilayers of tissuelike petals. Each stem bears several blooms atop fine, fernlike foliage. Ranunculus come in a) single or b) double flowering types.

2. Purchase or cut ranunculus when the blossoms are open but the petals are curved inward and still cupping the middle part of the flower. The flower should feel firm to the touch. The flower should not shed when handled.

3. Older ranunculus have petals that are more separated from the center. The tissuelike petals appear more transparent, with fading color. The flower is soft to the touch and may shed when handled.

4. Ranunculus have thin, hollow stems that break easily, which can make them difficult to arrange. Try inserting a wire into the stem, or brace the stem with a wire to support the flower. Ranunculus also droop because they have large heads atop their thin stems. A wire will also straighten the flower for better use in arrangements.

5. Two-tone or variegated types are called picotee ranunculus.

NAMES: Ranunculus, French or Persian Buttercup.
VARIETIES: *Ranunculus asiaticus* hybrids in single and double forms. The best variety for cut flowers is the tecolate strain, producing the finest and largest flowers.
COLORS: Available in most shades and colors, except no blue or black. They can have black or yellow centers. Some varieties are two-tone or striped. See photo 5.
SCENT: Mild scent.
FRESHNESS: Purchase or cut when the petals are cupping the middle of the flower and still fold inward.
VASE LIFE: 7 to 10 days or longer.
AVAILABILITY: Winter through spring, the predominant season being spring.
COSTS: Spring—moderately priced. Winter—moderately expensive.
MEANING: You are radiant!
ARRANGING TIP: Ranunculus stems break easily, making them difficult to arrange. See arranging tips 12, 13, 16, 17, 18, and 19.
GROWING TIP: Soaking ranunculus tubers for at least four hours before planting makes it easier for the tubers to root. They resemble claws and are sometimes called crow's feet. Plant them toes down. Ranunculus like cool nights and warm days with plenty of light. They can be grown as a garden flower and as a container flower.
OTHER: Ranunculus are heavy drinkers, so watch the water level. See care and conditioning tips 31, 32, 34, and 35.

1a

1b

1c

1d

2

1a, b, c, d. Roses, with their many layers of fragrant, velvet petals, are the most cherished and popular flowers of all times. There are hundreds of types and varieties of roses available as cut flowers and for growing. Some types are a) the traditional tea rose, which is most popular as a florist flower with medium to large well-formed blooms and long stems; b) the old-fashioned types, such as the cabbagehead roses or English roses, which are more delicate and fragrant than the commercial roses; c) the miniature rose, only about one inch across; and d) the spray rose, which consists of several branching small blossoms per stem.

2. Roses are so mass-produced that you must check the blossom carefully before purchasing. The shape and size of the head indicates which blooms will open properly. The bloom at left indicates a rose that has been cut too early. The blossom is bullet-shaped and very firm to the touch. Most people mistakenly prefer their roses this way, in hope of purchasing a fresher product and a long vase life. The petals are curved inward with no signs of opening. Roses of poor quality that are cut too early usually result in drooping heads. The bloom at right has a nice shape, with a few outer petals opening and the swirl of petals in the middle closed. It is somewhat firm to the touch with the feeling of several layers of petals to open.

1. Snapdragons are tall, vertical spike flowers with graduating clusters of velvety blossoms along the top part of the stem. They range from about two to three feet in height. A fresh snapdragon has some of its blossoms open on the bottom, with several developed buds closed toward the middle to the top. These buds show good color, and the tips are usually green with tight buds. The flowers are almost upright.

2. Older snapdragons have about two-thirds of their flowers open. Some of the bottom blossoms may be wilted or soft to the touch. The tip of the flower may start to droop. Snapdragons at this stage will still last several days if recleaned and cut shorter. The flower will then revive and last for several more days.

3. If you gently squeeze the side of a snapdragon blossom, you can see how this flower got its name. The blossoms resemble the mouth of a dragon, and the bottom lip will snap shut when released. This is actually how the flower protects its nectar. The pollinator must know how to open the blossom and get inside.

4. You can cut the tips off to encourage the blossoms to open sooner, but the closed blossoms and green tips offer interesting color and texture in arrangements. Here, the flowers are clumped together to form the base of the bouquet. Try this after the snapdragons are enjoyed as a taller flower, using the tips after some of the bottom blossoms are spent.

NAMES: Snapdragon, Antirrhinum.
COLORS: Shades of white, pink, apricot, yellow, deep red, and burgundy. Some have contrasting colors at the mouth of the blossom.
SCENT: Slight to none.
FRESHNESS: A few of the blossoms are open at the base of the flower spike, with the others in bud stage and showing good size and color. The flower is mostly upright.
AVAILABILITY: All year, but spring and summer are the peak seasons.
VASE LIFE: 10 days to 2 weeks.
COST: Inexpensive.
MEANING: Presumption.
ARRANGING TIP: Some suggest cutting the tips off to encourage more blossoms to open sooner. However, the tips add interesting color and texture. Also, see arranging tips 12, 13, 15, and 16.
GROWING TIP: A single snapdragon plant can be turned into several flowers by "fooling" the plant. When the snapdragon reaches two to four inches in height, pinch the stem back to the base of the plant. The plant will send up several new sprouts in response. See growing tip 17.
OTHER: See care and conditioning tips 8, 24, 32, 34, and 35.

1. Stock are sturdy spikes of dense clusters of sweetly scented single or double blossoms. Fresh stock have one-third to a half of their blossoms open, with the remaining buds showing good color and size.

2. Older stock have the bottom third of their flowers soft and wilted in appearance. Sometimes these blossoms have been stripped and only the middle and tip are left. Check the blossom count to make sure you are getting a fresh product. Stock should be six or more blossoms high.

3. Stock is useful as a base for arrangements, since the bottom part of the flower wilts first. Begin with a base of stock, adding other flowers in and around to hide the lower blossoms as the flower ages and leaving the middle part exposed. Stock also adds a lovely fragrance to any combination.

NAMES: Stock, Matthiola, Gillyflower.
COLORS: Pastel shades of white, pink, apricot, and yellow are most common, but deep pink and purple are also available.
SCENT: Strong, spicy clove scent.
FRESHNESS: One-third to one-half of the bottom blossoms are open, with the remaining buds showing good size and color.
VASE LIFE: 3 to 5 days.
AVAILABILITY: All year, but spring and summer are the peak seasons.
COST: Inexpensive.
MEANING: Lasting beauty.
ARRANGING TIP: Use this delightfully fragrant flower as a base for arrangements, so that the other flowers will hide the quickly spent bottom blossoms. The plump middle will make a nice addition for most combinations, their sturdy cushion appearance accenting other large flowers while acting as a brace for building the arrangement. See also arranging tips 12, 13, 14, and 15.
OTHER: Stock has very dense stems, which makes water penetration difficult and shortens the vase life of the flower. If the thick, white, fibrous base on the lower part of the stem remains, it must be cut away for proper conditioning. The fine fuzz that covers the stems contaminates the water and also shortens vase life. Change the water frequently and recut the ends. See also care and conditioning tips 4, 8, 24, and 32.

1a   1b   1c

2

3

4

1a, b, c. Sunflowers are showy, raylike flowers with large, disk-shaped centers. a) The most common type has bright golden petals and a dark-brown center. Other popular varieties are b) the double or teddy bear sunflower and c) the smaller, rust-colored or autumn beauty sunflower. Sunflowers may reach ten feet in height.

2. Purchase or cut sunflowers when three-fourths to fully open. The petals will still be slightly turned upward. The petals should be firm to the touch. The center is the best indication for freshness—there should be no pollen. Sunflowers produce quantities of yellow pollen with age, but some new, low-pollen varieties have a longer vase life.

3. Older sunflowers are fully open, with their petals turned downward. The petals are soft to the touch and may be bruised or may shed when handled. The middle shows signs of pollen formation.

4. If the petals are damaged or wilted, pull them off, away from the center, and use the deep-brown or green disk as an amusing texture accent.

NAMES: Sunflower, Helianthus.
VARIETIES: There are over a hundred varieties. *Helianthus annuus* (the common sunflower) in single and double varieties is the best known.
COLORS: All shades of yellow, from pale lemon to deep gold, are the most common. Some varieties are available in rust and brown colors. The disks may be brown or green in color.
SCENT: None.
FRESHNESS: Three-fourths to fully open, with the petals slightly turned upward and firm to the touch. The center disk is clean, with no signs of pollination. The flower is sturdy and upright.
VASE LIFE: Approximately 5 days. The large green leaves may wilt quickly after the flower is cut. Strip them away if necessary as this also prolongs vase life.
AVAILABILITY: Summer is the predominant season, but sunflowers are available in spring and fall as well.
COST: Moderately priced.
MEANING: Haughtiness, pride.
NOTE: Sunflowers are important for economic as well as decorative purposes, being used for oil production, seeds, dyes, in cosmetics, etc.
ARRANGING TIP: When the petals fade, separate them from the large disks and use the disks as an interesting touch in arrangements. See arranging tips 8, 14, and 17.
GROWING TIP: Start sunflower seed very early indoors, since from seed to flowering time is three to four months. Concentrate on the best seedlings, which are likely to develop sooner and produce the best flowers. See growing tip 20.
OTHER: Watch the water level—sunflowers are very heavy drinkers. See also care and conditioning tips 4, 8, 29, and 32.

1. Sweet peas grow on vines, each stem bearing five or more delicate, ruffled blossoms. Sweet peas should be cut or purchased when only a few of the bottom blossoms are fully open and some large, closed buds are ready to bloom at the top.

2. To cut or use sweet peas in arrangements, trim the stems away from the central vine at the base. The flowers will last longer when separated this way.

3. Sweet peas are easily damaged. Check blossoms closely for bruising or discoloration before purchasing.

4. With their beautiful ruffles, intense fragrance, and lovely colors, sweet peas add an exquisite old-fashioned touch to any bouquet. Use the vine foliage around the base of combinations for a more casual, natural look.

NAMES: Sweet Pea, Lathyrus Odoratus.
COLORS: White, cream, pinks, salmon, lavender, purple, and red. Some variegated and two-tone shades are also available.
SCENT: Very intense, sweet fragrance. Sweet pea oil is still used in making perfume.
FRESHNESS: A few flowers are fully open at the base of the stem, with several large blooms to open at the top.
VASE LIFE: 3 to 5 days.
AVAILABILITY: Midwinter into spring, sometimes summer in cooler climates.
COSTS: Winter—moderately expensive. Spring—moderately priced.
MEANING: Departure.
NOTE: Sweet pea seeds and flowers are poisonous.
ARRANGING TIP: These old-fashioned flowers, with their delicate ruffled petals, compelling fragrance, and fine colors, can be used alone or for adding a lacy touch to combinations. See also arranging tips 1, 8, and 12.
GROWING TIP: The more flowers you cut, the more blooms they offer. Soak sweet pea seeds for 24 hours before planting. They like warm days and cool nights for best bloom production, so plant accordingly. See growing tip 20.
OTHER: See care and conditioning tips 24 and 26.

1. Tulips are usually six-petaled, elongated cup-shaped flowers with slender stems and large, broad leaves. Purchase or cut tulips of good size and color, although a little green tinge is all right—they will continue to develop after cutting. The tulip should be firm to the touch, and upright. Check the inside of the blossoms for signs of pollen: The centers should be clean.

2. In aged tulips, the tips of the petals are discolored or have a transparent look. The center of the base shows signs of pollination, and the flower feels soft to the touch.

3. The so-called Dutch tulip on the right is a shorter variety with smaller blossom size than the French tulip on the left. The French tulips are longer lasting as a cut flower.

4a, b, c, d, e. Pictured here are a) striped or variegated Rembrandt tulips; b) lily or pencil tulips, with pointed petals; c) peony tulips, with double petals; d) parrot tulips, with ruffled petals; e) fringe tulips, with frayed edges.

5. When arranging with tulips, leave plenty of room, as they continue to grow and develop after being cut. They also open and close, and reach and move toward the light. Always set an arrangement with tulips in indirect light. Large tulip leaves can be gently curled and tucked between blossoms to keep flowers in place and allow you to use fewer of them.

NAMES: Tulip, Tulipa.
VARIETIES: There are 15 different divisions of tulips, with hundreds of species, the most common being the single tulip.
COLORS: All colors and combinations are available, except no true blue.
SCENT: A few varieties have a mild, sweet scent, but most have none.
FRESHNESS: Purchase or cut tulips when they show good size and color. A little green is fine. Tulips should be firm to the touch and upright. Check inside blossom to see that no pollen has developed.
VASE LIFE: About 5 days. The French variety will last 7 days or longer.
AVAILABILITY: January to May.
MEANING: Declaration of true love. "I am hopelessly in love with you."
COST: Winter—moderately priced. Spring—inexpensive. The French variety: Winter—expensive. Spring—moderately priced.
ARRANGING TIP: Tulips change daily after cutting. Leave enough room for tulips to grow and move, even if they are manipulated somewhat to fit into certain combinations. See arranging tips 1, 8, 10, 13, 17, 18, 19, and 20.
GROWING TIP: Tulips are easy to grow in the garden for spring color and can also be forced to bloom indoors in winter. They only bloom for a short time in the spring, so plant early-, mid-, and late-blooming varieties to extend tulip time. Most tulips become exhausted after a year or two, returning shorter and smaller every spring, so pick varieties that "naturalize" well. See growing tips 10, 11, and 12.
OTHER: Tulips are heavy drinkers! See care and conditioning tips 8, 23, 33, 34, and 35.

1. Snowball viburnums are round clusters of apple-green to pale-green branching flowers from thin, woody shrubs. Purchase or cut when the flower clusters are rather more green than white, the florets tight together, the cluster compact.

2. Older snowballs are a faded green to white in color. The florets are more open and separated, and they may shed when handled.

3. Viburnum shrubs produce attractive berries and fruit in the fall and winter. Some produce unusual steel-blue berries, which are handsome used in holiday arrangements.

4. Snowball viburnums are an excellent choice for tall combinations, their branching green clusters gently falling and draping. This is a good starter flower for building an arrangement, because the thick, woody stems create a maze in the container and the lush blossoms create a base at the top, which acts as a guide for adding other flowers. Viburnums can also be cut down and their blossoms used much like hydrangeas. See arranging tip 14 on page 39.

NAMES: Viburnum, Snowball.
VARIETIES: Viburnum Opulus varieties.
COLORS: Pale apple green to white shades.
SCENT: Slight fragrance.
FRESHNESS: The round clusters are dense and firm to the touch. The overall color is a light green, turning white with age.
VASE LIFE: 7 days, sometimes longer.
AVAILABILITY: Winter to mid-spring.
COST: Winter—expensive. Spring—moderately expensive.
ARRANGING TIP: Snowball viburnums are a useful tall, branching flower when building large arrangements. See photo 4. See also arranging tips 8, 12, 13, and 14.
OTHER: See care and conditioning tips 5, 6, 26, and 32.

1. Yarrows are flat, dense clusters of numerous small flowers atop graceful, fernlike foliage. The flowers within the cluster should be close together and upright. Fresh yarrows have most of their flowers open or just beginning to open. Cut in bud stage, they will not open.

2. On older yarrows the flowers on the cluster are more separated, with pollen forming. The flower may appear drooping and soft to the touch.

3. Yarrows are tall, graceful flowers to grow in the garden, where they are drought tolerant. Unfortunately, they do not perform like this as a cut flower; they wilt easily. Keep yarrows in deep water, or cut them down close to the base of the container to extend vase life. Yarrows make a colorful carpet with their flat heads for other flowers to rest upon.

NAMES: Yarrow, Achillea.
VARIETIES: Achillea Millefolium varieties.
COLORS: Shades of white, yellow, pink, peach, and red.
SCENT: Spicy scent similar to sage.
FRESHNESS: Most of the flowers are opening on the cluster.
VASE LIFE: Approximately 3 to 5 days.
AVAILABILITY: Summer into fall.
COST: Inexpensive.
MEANING: The flower of good health and well-being. Also, symbolic of healing.
NOTE: Yarrow has many uses, but is mostly associated with treating various health problems such as the common cold, stomach problems, and skin rashes.
ARRANGING TIP: Most varieties of yarrow wilt easily after cutting. Always use yarrow in deep water, or cut down close to the water source for some lasting power. The variety called "Coronation Gold" is a heartier variety that has a long vase life and will usually dry naturally and can be used out of water. See arranging tips 12 and 13.
GROWING TIP: Yarrow is a very easy and reliable perennial to grow. It thrives in poor soil conditions, drought, neglect, etc., and grows wild in many areas. Yarrow gives a natural, old-fashioned appearance to any garden or landscape. It loves the sun and attracts butterflies to the garden.
OTHER: Condition yarrow when cut in cool, deep water, foliage and all, for several hours. Also, see care and conditioning tips 32 and 34.

1. Zinnias are single- or double-petal daisy-type flowers that usually come in bold, bright colors. They have interesting, eye-catching centers with unusual details and contrasting colors. Zinnias are also available in other shapes and sizes, such as cactus, button, etc. See Dahlia for similar types.

2. Buy fresh zinnias when they are three-fourths to fully open. Cut too early, they will wilt prematurely. The color of the petals should be good and the flower upright and firm to the touch. The intricate, jewel-like middles should be clean, with little pollen formation. Zinnias bruise easily, so handle with care.

3. Older zinnias begin to brown around the edges of the petals, and the raylike petals appear to turn more downward. The petals may feel soft to the touch. The middle becomes more predominant as the pollen develops and the petals fold down.

NAME: Zinnia.
VARIETIES: *Zinnia elegans* varieties. Similar to dahlias in shapes and sizes. See page 76.
COLORS: All colors, shades, and combinations are available, except blue and black. Zinnias may be striped, two-tone, or multicolored.
SCENT: None.
FRESHNESS The flower is mostly open. Zinnias bruise easily.
VASE LIFE: Approximately 5 days, sometimes longer.
AVAILABILITY: Summer.
COST: Inexpensive.
MEANING: Thoughts of absent friends.
ARRANGING TIP: Zinnias are best used in arrangements when cut from the source, since they wilt easily if not cut at the proper stage. They have hollow stems that are prone to breaking and bending. See arranging tips 18 and 19.
GROWING TIP: Zinnias love hot weather. Do not bother to plant them early, as they will not do much until the temperature starts to climb. Zinnias are prone to mildew, so soak the roots beneath when watering, and try to avoid getting water on the flowers and foliage. Zinnias are fun to grow, with all their bright colors and amusing shapes. They are good in the garden, or can be grown in pots.

Acknowledgments

This book project requires many thanks to many people for their support, encouragement, and friendship. A special thanks to my very talented and patient photographer, T. K. Hill, and his support-ive wife, Angelique, for all the extra hours of work required to make the photographs for this book perfect.

The many great friends include Jeanne Maher, Sue and Allan Morris, and August Spier for believing in this project from start to finish. Tayloe and Mike Piggott, Kathy and Lee Gardner, Krista Anderson, Lee Ann Grant, Peg Invie, Pamela Periconi, Windland Smith Rice, Terry and Craig Durr.

A special thank you to Lois Sherr Dubin, who kindly introduced me to Margaret L. Kaplan, Senior Vice-President and Executive Editor at Harry N. Abrams, Inc., who encouraged me to do the book and provided counsel and enthusiasm along with editorial skill. Douglas Sardo also has my appreciation for his elegant organization of the visual materials and his invaluable assistance in art-directing the photography.

Thank you to my coworkers Elizabeth Mosley, Melissa Miller, Chelsea Jonke, and Kristin Hansen for all the hard work and support.

To my sister Lee Heffernan for all the encouraging words and support throughout the years, and especially with this project.

For all the beautiful flowers for the photographs, thank you to Will Fulton of Dos Osos Multifloro, Rita Brody of G. Page Wholesale, Jayne Hofer of Laloma Roses, and Bill Ludwig of Aard de Boer Flowers; other flower suppliers include Green Valley Growers, Amato Wholesale, and Virgin Farms.

And, finally, thanks to my best buddy Vincent for making me work toward and complete this goal.

The containers, tools, and supplies shown in this book are from Flower Hardware in Jackson Hole, Wyoming (307) 733-7040 or www.flowerhardware.com.

Editor: Margaret L. Kaplan
Designer: Douglas Sardo

Library of Congress Cataloging-in-Publication Data

Heffernan, Cecelia.
Flowers A to Z: buying, growing, cutting, arranging / Cecelia Heffernan; photography T. K. Hill.
p. cm.
ISBN 0–8109–3348–9 (hardcover) / ISBN 0–8109–9233–7 (pbk.)
1. Flowers. 2. Flower gardening. 3. Flower arrangement. I. Title.

SB405 .H44 2201
635.9'66—dc21   00–064282

Printed and bound in China
10 9 8 7 6 5 4 3 2 1

Harry N. Abrams, Inc.
100 Fifth Avenue
New York, N.Y. 10011
www.abramsbooks.com

Abrams is a subsidiary of

LA MARTINIÈRE
GROUPE